ADAPTING
UNSTOPPABLE
LEARNING

YAZMIN PINEDA ZAPATA   REBECCA BROOKS

Edited by Douglas Fisher and Nancy Frey

Solution Tree | Press

a division of
Solution Tree

555 North Morton Street
Bloomington, IN 47404
800.733.6786 (toll free) / 812.336.7700
FAX: 812.336.7790

email: info@SolutionTree.com
SolutionTree.com

Visit **go.SolutionTree.com/instruction** to download the free reproducibles in this book.

Printed in the United States of America

21 20 19 18 17   1 2 3 4 5

Library of Congress Cataloging-in-Publication Data

Names: Zapata, Yazmin Pineda, author. | Brooks, Rebecca, 1974- author. |
  Fisher, Douglas, editor. | Frey, Nancy, 1959- editor. | Fisher, Douglas,
  1965- related work. Unstoppable learning,
Title: Adapting Unstoppable learning / Yazmin Pineda Zapata and Rebecca
  Brooks ; editors, Douglas Fisher and Nancy Frey.
Description: Bloomington, IN : Solution Tree Press, [2017] | Includes
  bibliographical references and index.
Identifiers: LCCN 2017002724 | ISBN 9781943874217 (perfect bound)
Subjects: LCSH: Children with disabilities--Education. | Individualized
  instruction. | Learning strategies.
Classification: LCC LC4015 .Z27 2017 | DDC 371.9--dc23 LC record available at https://lccn.loc.
gov/2017002724

Solution Tree
Jeffrey C. Jones, CEO
Edmund M. Ackerman, President

Solution Tree Press
President and Publisher: Douglas M. Rife
Editorial Director: Sarah Payne-Mills
Managing Production Editor: Caroline Weiss
Senior Production Editor: Tonya Maddox Cupp
Senior Editor: Amy Rubenstein
Copy Editor: Miranda Addonizio
Proofreader: Kendra Slayton
Text and Cover Designer: Laura Cox
Editorial Assistants: Jessi Finn and Kendra Slayton

Acknowledgments

This book is dedicated to all of the inspiring students and dedicated staff who have embarked with us on this journey to support and advocate for inclusive schooling to ensure equitable education for all students.

The authors would like to acknowledge the valuable contributions of:

Broc Arnaiz, general educator

Joseph Assof, mathematics teacher

Danielle Carlin, English teacher

Elizabeth Castagnera, special educator

Arturo Cuevas, mathematics teacher

Kim Elliot, biology teacher

Susana Jimenez, paraprofessional

Ashlee Montferret, special educator

Solution Tree Press would like to thank the following reviewers:

Sari Fensterheim
IEP Coordinator, Testing Coordinator, and Reading Recovery Teacher
PS 58 The Carroll School
Brooklyn, New York

Samantha McMasters
Director of Special Education
Bexley City School District
Bexley, Ohio

Jessica Murphy
Director of Special Education
Concord Public Schools
Concord, Massachusetts

Tracy Tamillo
Teacher of Students Who Are Deaf or Hard of Hearing
West Central Education District
Sauk Centre, Minnesota

Cynthia Trinidad
IEP Coordinator
East Bridgewater Junior/Senior High School
East Bridgewater, Massachusetts

Visit **go.SolutionTree.com/instruction** to download the free reproducibles in this book.

Table of Contents

About the Editors. vii

About the Authors ix

Foreword xi
    By Douglas Fisher and Nancy Frey

Introduction. 1
    About Adapting Learning 1
    About This Book's Underpinnings 2
    About This Book's Student Beneficiaries 7
    About This Book's Readers 7
    About Using This Book as a Resource. 8

1 Creating an Adaptation-Friendly Systems Thinking Classroom 11
    Systems Thinking 11
    Triangle of Support 15
    Universal Design for Learning 15
    The Takeaways 29

2 Making Accommodations and Modifications While Ensuring Rigor . 31
    Accommodations. 33
    Modifications 46
    Adaptations as Accommodations or Modifications 47
    Rigor 49
    The Takeaways 51

3 Determining Personal Supports 53
    Full-Time Support. 53
    Part-Time Support 54

Intermittent Support 54

Peer Tutor Support 54

Natural Support 56

Supplemental Support 56

Co-Teaching 57

The Takeaways 58

4 Communicating With Key Collaborators 59

Naming Key Collaborators. 60

Sharing Responsibility. 63

The Takeaways 67

Epilogue: Changing a Belief System 69

References and Resources 71

Index 75

About the Editors

 **Douglas Fisher, PhD,** is professor of educational leadership at San Diego State University and a teacher leader at Health Sciences High and Middle College. He teaches courses in instructional improvement and formative assessment. As a classroom teacher, Fisher focuses on English language arts instruction. He was director of professional development for the City Heights Educational Collaborative and also taught English at Hoover High School.

Fisher received an International Reading Association Celebrate Literacy Award for his work on literacy leadership. For his work as codirector of the City Heights Professional Development Schools, Fisher received the Christa McAuliffe Award. He was corecipient of the Farmer Award for excellence in writing from the National Council of Teachers of English (NCTE) as well as the 2014 Exemplary Leader for the Conference on English Leadership, also from NCTE.

Fisher has written numerous articles on reading and literacy, differentiated instruction, and curriculum design. His books include *Teaching Students to Read Like Detectives*, *Checking for Understanding*, *Better Learning Through Structured Teaching*, and *Rigorous Reading*.

He earned a bachelor's degree in communication, a master's degree in public health, an executive master's degree in business, and a doctoral degree in multicultural education. Fisher completed postdoctoral study at the National Association of State Boards of Education focused on standards-based reforms.

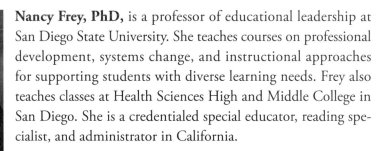

Nancy Frey, PhD, is a professor of educational leadership at San Diego State University. She teaches courses on professional development, systems change, and instructional approaches for supporting students with diverse learning needs. Frey also teaches classes at Health Sciences High and Middle College in San Diego. She is a credentialed special educator, reading specialist, and administrator in California.

Before joining the university faculty, Frey was a public school teacher in Florida. She worked at the state level for the Florida Inclusion Network, helping districts design systems for supporting students with disabilities in general education classrooms.

She is the recipient of the 2008 Early Career Achievement Award from the Literacy Research Association and the Christa McAuliffe Award for excellence in teacher education from the American Association of State Colleges and Universities. She was corecipient of the Farmer Award for excellence in writing from the National Council of Teachers of English for the article "Using Graphic Novels, Anime, and the Internet in an Urban High School."

Frey is coauthor of *Text-Dependent Questions*, *Using Data to Focus Instructional Improvement*, and *Text Complexity: Raising Rigor in Reading.* She has written articles for *The Reading Teacher*, *Journal of Adolescent and Adult Literacy*, *English Journal*, *Voices in the Middle*, *Middle School Journal*, *Remedial and Special Education*, and *Educational Leadership*.

To book Douglas Fisher or Nancy Frey for professional development, contact pd@SolutionTree.com.

About the Authors

Yazmin Pineda Zapata, EdD, is a program specialist and teacher leader at Health Sciences High and Middle College in San Diego, California. Her expertise in delivering special education services has allowed her to advocate for students with varying learning differences in grades K–12. Yazmin is credentialed as an administrator, a teacher in multiple subjects, and an education specialist for students with mild to moderate and moderate to severe disabilities.

Yazmin mentors teacher candidates completing credentials in special education as a cooperating teacher and also supports school districts and nonprofit organizations across the nation to implement appropriate curriculum adaptations that provide equitable access to all learners. She actively presents and consults in the areas of best practices for accessible curriculum, co-teaching, collaborative planning, and inclusive education.

Yazmin has a bachelor's degree in English literature and language, a master's degree in special education with an emphasis in curriculum, and a doctoral degree in educational leadership.

Rebecca Brooks, PhD, is an assistant professor in the special education teacher preparation and graduate program in the School of Education at California State University San Marcos. Prior to joining the university faculty, Rebecca was a public school special educator for grades K–12 serving the role of an inclusion support teacher. She has worked with individuals with developmental disabilities in educational, recreational, vocational, and residential settings for more than twenty-five years.

She is a nationwide presenter and consultant in the areas of best practices for inclusive education and peer tutoring support systems. She has written journal articles on inclusive education and peer tutoring and coauthored the book *Peer Tutoring and*

Support: Making Inclusive Education Work. She has her multiple subjects and education specialist teaching credentials. She is also a Leading Edge Certified (LEC) online and blended learning teacher.

Rebecca earned an associate's degree in developmental disabilities, a bachelor's degree in communicative disorders, a master's degree in education with an emphasis in special education, and a doctoral degree in education with a focus on social justice.

To book Yazmin Pineda Zapata or Rebecca Brooks for professional development, contact pd@SolutionTree.com.

Foreword

By Douglas Fisher and Nancy Frey

Education begs for equity. In 1975, Congress passed Public Law 94–142 (Education for All Handicapped Children Act, 1975), ensuring that youth with disabilities could attend school. Ten years before that, Congress passed the first version of the Elementary and Secondary Education Act (1965), whose current version is known as the Every Student Succeeds Act, or ESSA (2015). These acts increase efforts for students who live in poverty as well as those who struggle with school. The stage was set, legally, for students with disabilities to receive a free and appropriate public education. School systems work to educate students to the maximum extent possible, with appropriate supports and services.

Before continuing, we should let you know that we have been labeled radical inclusionists. That label makes us proud even though those who label us do so disparagingly. We believe so strongly that students with and without disabilities should be educated together that in 2007, we started a new high school where exactly that occurs. We strongly support inclusion and believe that the regular classroom is the least restrictive environment. Providing students what they need to be successful is the right thing to do.

But simply placing students who struggle in general education classes without support dooms them to fail. Congress knew that back in 1975, and many educators are still learning that lesson today. Many learning environments are not conducive to the success of students who struggle with learning or physical disabilities, which is where curriculum and technology support come into play. Some students also need support with behavior, personal care, health, and so on. Some students simply struggle with one topic during an entire academic year's worth of topics. The fact is, the law requires that school systems provide support so that students can be successful in the general classroom. Educators have to design appropriate supports and services before recommending that a student be considered for an alternative environment.

Of course, our collective understanding of how to support students who struggle has changed considerably. Over the past several decades, there have been breakthroughs for developing accommodations and modifications. This book contains relevant, current information about the techniques that general and special educators can use to support students' learning needs. It's full of tried and true approaches, as well as new technologies, for supporting students in the general classroom.

Importantly, when done well, the positive effects of accommodations and supports for struggling students spill over and impact other students. We have seen countless students better understand a complex concept after seeing the modified version of the learning target. We also have seen teachers change their lessons based on the accommodations that were intended for students. Sometimes, the accommodations and modifications are better than the original curriculum and everyone learns more—but that's not the main goal of providing curricular, personal, or technological support. The real intention is curriculum accessibility for all students, and that depends on educators having sufficient knowledge to design and redesign learning tasks that all students can access.

It is important that the accommodations and modifications ensure that the tasks remain challenging but not out of reach. That's a delicate balance that Yazmin Pineda Zapata and Rebecca Brooks tackle with skill. They provide a wide range of both imagined and real-life examples and ideas that educators can apply to ensure that students receiving support are accountable for their learning and that the support team maintains high expectations and rigor. This book contains the tools that educators need to make learning unstoppable for all students.

Introduction

An educator's task is not only to make curriculum engaging but to ensure that all learners can access that curriculum. All teachers want to design beautiful lessons packed with insightful material and multifaceted activities, but that is not enough if the assessment shows that multiple students have not mastered the concepts. Reteaching a lesson is a reactive solution; this book helps teachers proactively ensure education equity. But what is equity in education? It is not the same as equality, which means providing the same instruction and support for everyone. Equal divvying of resources may result in a fair education for all students, but "fair is not always equal" according to authors Richard L. Curwin and Allen N. Mendler (1988, p. 31).

Providing an *equitable* education means focusing on meeting each student's individual needs, considering the whole student and the multitude of contexts in which his or her needs change. To do so, educators must recognize and alter the existing structures and practices within classrooms—how they provide support and teach content, for example—thereby adapting learning to meet those needs. Education research further highlights the need for all educators to embrace the idea of all students having access to the general education curriculum, and that approach requires equity (Crockett, 2011; Shepherd & Hasazi, 2008). What does adapting learning entail? The following section explains.

About Adapting Learning

Adaptations include any support, change, or alteration that allows students to access any part of their school day. They differentiate instruction and come in a variety of forms: curriculum changes, support that staff or peers provide, technology devices, or environment changes. Two education approaches fall under the adaptations umbrella. *Accommodations* supply students with the tools and strategies they need to access curriculum: content, standards, instructional level, and performance criteria, while lessons remain unchanged. In contrast, *modifications* change the curriculum and objectives and adjust the standards (Fisher & Frey, 2015). Accommodations and modifications are both differentiation.

Accommodations can take the form of environmental changes (such as dimming lights) or activity changes (such as oral versus written directions). Modifications take the form of, for example, changing, "Compare and contrast two or more characters, settings, or events in a story or drama, drawing on specific details in the text (e.g., how characters interact)" (RL. 5.3) to "Identify and describe one character, setting or event in a story or drama, drawing on specific details in the text (for example, what the character looks like)" (National Governors Association Center for Best Practices & Council of Chief State School Officers [NGA & CCSSO], 2010). This book focuses on accommodations as well as modifications, offering real-world examples set in the classroom and the teacher's lounge.

The terms *accommodation* and *modification* are often used together or inter-changeably. This book will purposefully use them in accordance with the definitions we've given, even though one can debate whether a specific change or support is an accommodation versus a modification. Systems thinking, the basis for Unstoppable Learning that we explain in chapter 1 (page 11), compels educators to focus not on terminology, but on the big picture: Are all students getting what they need to succeed?

Adapting Unstoppable Learning helps educators give students what they need by espousing the principles in Douglas Fisher's and Nancy Frey's (2015) *Unstoppable Learning* and then bundling them with the so-called triangle of support and universal design for learning.

About This Book's Underpinnings

Important concepts support the wide scope of learning adaptations and equitable education. Those concepts include systems thinking (a tenet of unstoppable learning), the triangle of support, and universal design for learning. The following subsections explain each concept and how the triangle of support and universal design for learning lead back to and invariably depend on systems thinking.

Systems Thinking

Unstoppable Learning comprises seven elements that Fisher and Frey (2015) consider essential: (1) planning, (2) launching, (3) consolidating, (4) assessing, (5) adapting, (6) managing, and (7) leading. This book, *Adapting Unstoppable Learning*, focuses on the fifth element. Unstoppable Learning requires that educators infuse each of these elements with systems thinking. Fisher and Frey (2015) explain the concept best: "Systems thinking is the ability to see the big picture, observe how the elements within a system influence one another, identify emerging patterns, and act on them in ways that fortify the structures within" (p. 2). Four principles gird the effective systems thinking classroom: (1) relationships, (2) communication, (3) responsiveness, and (4) sustainability (Fisher & Frey, 2015). Figure I.1 shows the components and principles of Unstoppable Learning.

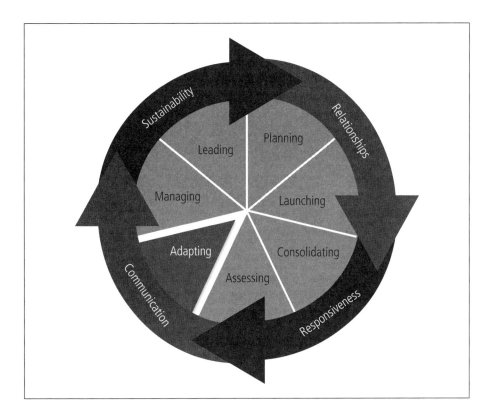

Source: Fisher & Frey, 2015.

Figure I.1: Unstoppable Learning components.

Driving questions direct both classroom instruction and student supports. Fisher and Frey (2015), in *Unstoppable Learning*, pose driving questions for learning adaptations, and we answer those questions and others in feature boxes and throughout the text.

- How can I leverage structures to improve learning?
- Have I checked the results of my curriculum and instruction and taken action to ensure successive approximation?
- What are the short-term and long-term consequences of the adaptations I provide for students? (p. 177)

Structures, curriculum, and adaptations, integral in applying systems thinking, are precisely what the triangle of support addresses. We explain that next.

Triangle of Support

How do educators determine what areas need special attention when a student requires accommodations? The triangle of support names three key areas to focus on, and they reflect the big-picture consideration that systems thinkers require: (1) personal supports, (2) curriculum adaptations, and (3) instructional and assistive technology (Castagnera, Fisher, Rodifer, Sax, & Frey, 2003).

Figure I.2 displays a graphic representation of the triangle of support. Chapter 2 (page 31) looks at these supports in greater detail.

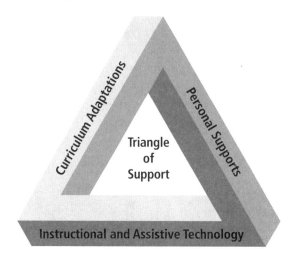

Source: Adapted from Castagnera et al., 2003.

Figure I.2: The triangle of support.

We rely on the triangle of support because in our experience as K–12 educators, some form of support is often lacking when students struggle to access the general education curriculum and meet standards. The triangle of support consistently and accurately guides the key areas worth considering. Personal supports include personal assistance and prompting. Curriculum adaptions allow students to have content and materials made accessible for them by tailoring to their learning needs and styles. A wealth of instructional and assistive technology provides access in a variety of innovative ways.

Universal Design for Learning

Universal design for learning is "a process that maximizes learning for all students, minimizes the need for individual accommodations, and eventually benefits every learner by considering different ways that students' minds are activated" (Hunt & Andreasen, 2011, p. 168). The universal design for learning framework requires educators to analyze the most effective input and output methods for student instruction and assessment. *Input* is how students receive information, and *output* is how students demonstrate what they have learned. The student profile, infused skills grid, and academic unit lesson plan are tools that aid that analysis. You will find exemplars for tool use in chapter 1 (page 11). Once teachers have used these tools for their analysis, they can funnel the information into the three crucial aspects of universal design for learning: representation, expression, and engagement. Figure I.3 displays a graphic representation of this funneling into universal design for learning, and we discuss it in more detail in chapter 1.

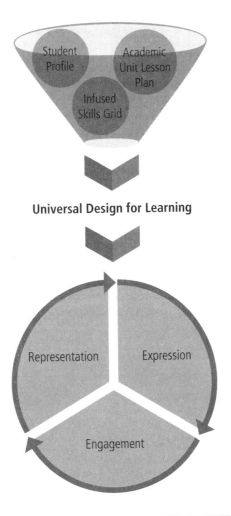

Figure I.3: Universal design for learning.

An Elegant Melding

The elegant melding of systems thinking, the triangle of support, and universal design for learning forms a fortified learning environment where students do not have to be concerned with how they will access the curriculum they encounter and instead can focus on enjoying the process. They receive the tools they need to be successful.

The systems thinking approach intertwines with the triangle of support when educators purposefully develop meaningful *relationships* with the key players on a student's education team while maintaining consistent *communication*. Alertness to learners' constant changes, which we define as educator *responsiveness*, fosters a *sustainable* foundation from which educators can build student success in learning. Incorporating universal design for learning into purposeful planning allows the education team to anticipate struggles, consider differentiated instruction, and evaluate the need for additional adaptations. Teachers can accomplish this by embedding differentiation methods and other adaptations into the curriculum and lesson design from the beginning. Implementing universal design for learning provides the opportunity to differentiate and adapt the representation, expression, and engagement of any instructional activity.

Using universal design for learning principles in lesson planning, as well as in the areas that the triangle of support identifies (personal supports, curriculum adaptations, and instructional and assistive technology), allows educators to see that there are various ways to meet the same learning target. Universal design for learning implements the best way for all students to have access, requiring educators to explore ways for all students to reach the same goal. Educating students is about allowing them to explore their own learning styles, exposing them to not only content knowledge but knowledge of how they learn best and the supports that best help them. Teachers can provide a supportive learning environment through systems thinking, reflecting, and focusing on how they can best adapt instruction to reach all learners—to make it universal. Figure I.4 is a graphic representation of how teachers can ensconce universal design for learning and the triangle of support within systems thinking.

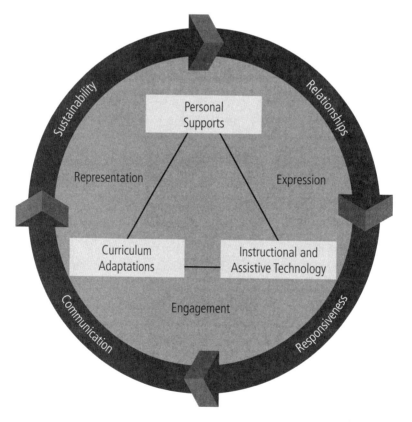

Source: Adapted from Castagnera et al., 2003; Fisher & Frey, 2015.

Figure I.4: Unstoppable Learning, the triangle of support, and universal design for learning melded.

About This Book's Student Beneficiaries

Though teachers often consider adaptations for students with disabilities, adaptations are not solely provided to students receiving special education services. Some students simply struggle with certain concepts. All students can benefit. In fact, Tracey E. Hall, Anne Meyer, and David H. Rose (2012) declare:

> One of the clearest and most important revelations stemming from brain research is that there are no "regular" students. The notion of broad categories of learners—"smart–not smart," "disabled–not disabled," "regular–not regular"—is a gross oversimplification that does not reflect reality. By categorizing students in this way, we miss many subtle and important qualities and strengths. (p. 2)

With this end in mind, educators must acknowledge a variety of considerations when implementing instruction, activities, and tests, and keep rigor intact. The examples in this book, for instance, are from our professional classroom experience with actual students. The existence of various learning differences and styles, disabilities, cultures, languages, and home-life challenges calls for educators to implement culturally responsive pedagogy that facilitates adaptations in the classroom.

These types of instructional decisions are complex. Systems thinking requires that educators make these decisions while considering all issues. Regardless of the challenges, the central focus should be on what best serves the student. We reiterate that equality refers to sameness. It's equity that should be at the forefront to ensure that teachers account for and address differences.

About This Book's Readers

This book is for general K–12 teachers, special education teachers, instructional assistants, paraprofessionals, and related service providers including but not limited to speech-language pathologists, counselors and psychologists, occupational and physical therapists, assistive technology specialists, audiology and mobility specialists, and deaf and hard-of-hearing specialists. These educators work with students who need adaptations, though not all students who need adaptations require staff support in addition to their classroom teacher. Communication, integral to systems thinking, becomes crucial to teaching via teams.

Administrators and district leaders who read this book and embrace the systems thinking mindset—focusing on relationships, responsiveness, communication, and sustainability—will clearly see that learning adaptations are not a place, a label, or a particular person. They are accommodations, modifications, and supports that meet students where they are. Making this shift in thinking allows all stakeholders to see adapting learning as an integral part of students' learning experiences and to see the school community as a place where everyone can reap the benefits of a supportive classroom environment.

About Using This Book as a Resource

It's important to note that when integrating accommodations and modifications, teachers must keep in mind any existing guidelines for determining how adaptations may affect students meeting graduation requirements and attaining a diploma. For those students, ensure that the provided adaptations do not alter the standards for the curriculum and that students who are receiving these supports are meeting their school's course requirements. The question of whether the chosen adaptation changes the standards determines if it is an accommodation or a modification. Universal design for learning and accommodations that do not alter the standards provide an array of supports for students receiving a diploma.

In any respect, this book provides real-life examples and explains what adaptations an education team needs to provide for the variety of ways students learn. It highlights the intersection of Fisher and Frey's (2015) systems thinking approach with adapted learning. Chapter 1, "Creating an Adaptation-Friendly Systems Thinking Classroom," further discusses the principles that underlie systems thinking and, hence, Unstoppable Learning. The chapter also explores the triangle of support and universal design for learning tools, which blend with systems thinking to direct educators as they create equitable adaptations. Chapter 2, "Making Accommodations and Modifications While Ensuring Rigor," details specific adaptations and explores gifted and *twice-exceptional* learners (learners who have giftedness and a disability). We discuss the different levels at and forms in which staff and peers can provide support in chapter 3, "Determining Personal Supports." To that end, chapter 4, "Communicating With Key Collaborators," considers the various stakeholders who co-plan together to design learning adaptations.

The driving questions that Fisher and Frey (2015) pose in *Unstoppable Learning* encourage educators to think deeply about their own curriculum design and presentation and the way students demonstrate their knowledge and skills. These driving questions appear in feature boxes throughout this book to take readers on an inquiry-based path to explore their pedagogical philosophy. Here are just a few of the questions that educators will answer in the course of reading *Adapting Unstoppable Learning*.

- What adaptations can I make to assignments and classroom activities?
- What tools facilitate universally designed lessons and support system implementation?
- How can I make adaptations while maintaining rigor?

- How can I integrate personal supports and technology into my classroom?

This books also aims to supply readers with a deep understanding of curriculum, personal, and technological supports. Three useful forms—(1) student profile, (2) infused skills grid, and (3) academic unit lesson plan—guide the reader through creating meaningful, effective adaptations. Numerous strategy examples provide readers with ideas to design an accessible lesson. It is our hope that this book provides educators with the tools necessary to teach and support all students.

CHAPTER 1

CREATING AN ADAPTATION-FRIENDLY SYSTEMS THINKING CLASSROOM

The systems thinking that creates Unstoppable Learning is integral to providing adaptations for students. Systems thinking compels educators to see the big picture and make decisions that benefit students as a learning body. Applying this thinking leads educators to the triangle of support and universal design for learning. These two key methods take a broad look at classroom needs and use specific elements within a lesson to build a fortified platform that ensures students comprehend and meet learning targets. To make these elements work together successfully and craft the content, process, and products, educators must commit to systems thinking and use the triangle of support and universal design for learning as guides to help them ensure that students receive what they need.

Systems Thinking

The educator is responsible for detecting patterns, new and recurring, so he or she can strengthen the structures that help a classroom run effectively (Fisher & Frey, 2015). Creating an effective learning environment also is characterized by an educator's ability to identify the barriers students face and strategize the elements of a lesson to overcome those obstacles. In a systems thinking classroom and school community, all stakeholders understand that it takes a collaborative effort to ensure each student's learning success. All stakeholders must remain aware that many elements and structures interweave and develop a thriving learning environment that responds to these interactions.

Fisher and Frey (2015) introduce the concept of *systems thinking* as a way educators "recognize the dynamic nature of the organized groups they operate within and . . . activate the right elements at the right time to reach the desired outcome" (p. 2). Within a school, a systems thinker views the classroom as a whole and meticulously identifies how various elements influence that system. The four systems thinking principles—(1) relationships, (2) communication, (3) responsiveness, and (4) sustainability—are integral to providing learning adaptations (Fisher & Frey, 2015).

Consider the importance of relationships among students and education team members (including paraprofessionals, related service providers, and families). Open lines of communication in these relationships ensure that educators are responsive to students. A sensibility for developing and maintaining relationships, engaging in ongoing communication, and being responsive brings educators full circle with sustainability as the capstone. These principles, which are discussed in the following sections, are essential to creating a culture amenable to learning adaptations within a systems thinking classroom.

Relationships

Teachers are ideally sensitive to dynamic personalities in their classrooms and strive to nurture positive relationships and maintain a safe learning climate for all students. Jason J. Teven and James C. McCroskey (1997) report that the level to which students believe their teachers care about them affects how those students perceive their own learning. Certainly, through natural human instinct, we understand how critical our interpersonal relationships and communication are to both the teaching and learning processes and the socioemotional development of students (American Psychological Association, Coalition for Psychology in Schools and Education, 2015). This communication embodies many facets of teachers' relationships with students, since thoughts and feelings become clear with verbal and nonverbal cues. To develop a safe environment, both physically and emotionally, teachers must establish a foundation of clear and genuine communication that continually nurtures a teacher-student relationship. Educators may create an inclusive, supportive culture by greeting all students daily by their first names, touching base with students when they return from an absence, noticing students' emotional and physical states and addressing them as needed, and getting to know each student's interests and aspirations. Building supportive relationships with students is impossible without communication.

Communication

Communication applies to all aspects of the learning environment up to and including the classroom's physical features. Not only do verbal directions and admonitions convey what is important to students, but so do wall posters and daily routines. When engaging in verbal communication, teachers can focus on language that encourages students to see how their learning applies beyond the classroom. Seeing how content relates to their own lives can increase relevance, which deepens understanding and future knowledge application (Roberson, 2013). Presenting concrete personal examples is a common accommodation. For example, while reading Upton

Sinclair's *The Jungle*, a book that highlights the unsanitary practices in the American meat-packing industry during the early 20th century, the teacher can discuss current restaurant cleanliness grades (A, B, C), since students encounter that food safety language in their community. Both the teacher and student should also prioritize clear and specific academic language. Teachers can support students in using academic language during small-group and whole-group opportunities by modeling; pairing students who will learn from each other; and encouraging repeated oral practice with sentence starters or frames.

Communication evolves between educators and students as relationships form in the classroom. This evolution motivates students to communicate more personally, sharing insights into how life outside school may affect their performance in school. This information can inform the need for and the necessary type of adaptations. In addition, each activity in a classroom will lead a student to interpret the learning in a slightly different manner, which again highlights the constant need for communication regarding both a student's academic and home life.

Educator-to-educator communication is as important as student-to-educator communication. Some students require more support staff, including related service providers. Whatever the team size, communication about the student's progress toward learning goals is crucial. Chapter 4 (page 59) lays out potential team members and ideas for successful collaboration. One outcome of this communication is a team's responsiveness.

Responsiveness

Responsiveness is one of the systems thinking principles that educators can apply to all aspects of the learning environment—especially the critical component of instruction. Systems thinking requires purposeful planning. A teacher's ability to provide differentiated instruction depends on his or her planning with the full range of abilities in mind before delivering the lesson in the classroom. Hall, Vue, Strangman, and Meyer (2014) explain that "to differentiate instruction is to recognize students' varying background knowledge, readiness, language, preferences in learning and interests; and to react responsively" (p. 3). Differentiated instruction is therefore a process of adapting learning by using a variety of accommodations and modifications in the following three areas as needed: teaching, learning activities, and student (coursework) requirements (California Services for Technical Assistance and Training, 2013). Tomlinson (2014) suggests that educators ask what it will take to adapt curriculum and instruction so that each learner gains the knowledge and skills required to succeed. A systematic way of providing differentiated instruction for students who are struggling is known as a multitiered system of supports (MTSS). MTSS includes response to instruction and intervention (RTI[2]), which is a multitiered, data-driven intervention approach to helping students achieve standards.

This differentiation ensures rigor for every student, whatever adaptation is made. These teachers plan contingencies as well. Given students' dynamism, systems thinkers must respond to their changing needs and their myriad instruction interpretations. These responses are crucial to providing academic support through adaptations. The classroom environment evolves, and each student constantly changes. Therefore, teachers must be ready to adapt their classrooms and instruction. As the year progresses, the systems thinking teacher anticipates and responds to specific student needs by way of the relationships and communication he or she has with students and educational team members.

Sustainability

Sustainability cycles back to the other key principles of a systems thinking approach, where it is evident that building relationships on communication and deliberate responsiveness to students is vital for establishing consistent growth. Therefore, consistent, equitable structure and support for all learners creates sustainability, which is imperative not only within the four walls of a teacher's domain but within the school system to which all members belong. Adaptations are unsustainable if teachers implement them on the fly or if not all teachers implement them, especially in schools where students travel from class to class.

Staff and funding changes can directly impact supports' systemic sustainability. Through collaboration with staff and administration, educators must determine how to maintain structured supports as systemic changes occur. Creative planning and forethought allow for proactive planning, such as using readily available resources (like peers) and sharing the responsibilities of adaptations amongst staff to maintain lasting support. Sustainability is key to a systems thinking classroom.

What Adaptations Do I Need to Provide for Specific Students?

Educators must ask themselves, "What is this particular assignment's objective? What is the objective for this specific student?" The answers to those questions will help teachers determine how to differentiate instruction and whether to introduce accommodations or modifications and, if so, what to provide to the student. When designing lessons in collaboration with a myriad of educators and support staff, the insight and feedback from all participating individuals will provide necessary information as well. Related service providers bring their ideas to address specific needs into the general education curriculum so adaptations can occur in those areas. For example, special educators, reading specialists, and English learner instructors will share their expertise, experience, and successful former strategies, whether in general or with a particular student. Teachers should also feel comfortable communicating with students' previous teachers to inquire about what adaptions were successful in the past.

Triangle of Support

As we noted in this book's introduction, the triangle of support encompasses three areas: (1) personal supports, (2) curriculum accommodations and modifications, and (3) instructional and assistive technology (Castagnera et al., 2003). Differentiated instruction, which is based on individual learners' needs, may employ any area of the triangle of support at any given time.

Personal Supports

Personal supports include anyone on a student's support team, including classroom teachers, paraprofessionals, and specialists, as well as his or her peers. Personal supports come in different levels, including full time, part time, and intermittent; peer tutors; natural supports (students); and supplemental supports. The type, frequency, and support level vary by student. We explain personal supports in much greater detail in chapter 3 (page 53).

Curriculum Adaptations

Curriculum adaptations allow all students, not just those with disabilities, to participate and perform successfully in all lesson activities. Some brief examples of curriculum accommodations include calculator use, teacher-supplied notes, highlighted text, problems broken into steps, a scribe, and visual aids. Modifications change the curriculum to the point of changing standards. Chapter 2 (page 31) reveals more options and discusses when they work best. While technology provides many supports in and of itself, teachers can use technology to provide curriculum adaptations.

Instructional and Assistive Technology

The third component, instructional and assistive technology, facilitates access to the instruction itself or how the student demonstrates competency, or supports a student's functional capabilities. It assists students as they learn or undergo assessment. This component comprises high-tech and low-tech supports. *High-tech supports* include but are not limited to word-prediction software, alternative keyboards, and augmentative communication devices. *Low-tech supports* include usually less expensive accommodations that don't require batteries, such as pencil grips, writing props, and graph paper. Teachers can explore fine and gross motor supports, educational aids, communication tools, and specific websites. Chapter 2 provides detailed examples and explanations.

Universal Design for Learning

Universal design for learning stems from designers considering consumers' architectural, engineering, and environmental needs (Connell et al., 1997). Architects, product designers, engineers, and environmental design researchers at the Center for

Universal Design (CUD) established seven principles of universal design. Educators can apply these principles, listed in table 1.1, when designing lectures, class discussions, group work, handouts, web-based instruction, fieldwork, and other academic activities (Connell et al., 1997).

Table 1.1: Universal Design Principles

Principle	Definition	Classroom Example
Equitable use	"The design is useful and [viable] to people with diverse abilities" (Connell et al., 1997).	Design a classroom website that is accessible to students who use text-to-speech software (Burgstahler, 2015).
Flexibility in use	"[An activity] design accommodates a wide range of individual preferences and abilities" (Connell et al., 1997).	Let students choose between reading or listening to a description of classroom station instructions (Burgstahler, 2015).
Simple and intuitive	"Use of the design is easy to understand, regardless of the user's experience, knowledge, language skills, or current concentration level" (Connell et al., 1997).	Label controls on microscopes with intuitive text and symbols (Burgstahler, 2015).
Perceptible information	"The design communicates necessary information effectively to the user, regardless of ambient conditions or the user's sensory abilities" (Connell et al., 1997).	Screen a video that has closed captioning (Burgstahler, 2015).
Tolerance for error	"The design minimizes hazards and the adverse consequences of accidental or unintended actions" (Connell et al., 1997).	Provide software that offers background information and guides student responses (Burgstahler, 2015).
Low physical effort	"The design can be used efficiently and comfortably and with minimal fatigue" (Connell et al., 1997).	Ensure that the school has doors that open automatically (Burgstahler, 2015).
Size and space for approach and use	"Appropriate size and space is provided for approach, reach, manipulation, and use regardless of the [student's] body size, posture, or mobility" (Connell et al., 1997).	Ensure the work space accommodates students who are left- or right-handed, as well as students who work while standing (Burgstahler, 2015).

Source: Burgstahler, 2015; Connell et al., 1997.

The Center for Applied Special Technology (CAST) is the nonprofit organization that has most ubiquitously applied the seven universal design principles to education in schools. Universal design for learning makes content accessible to students with a wide range of abilities, language skills, and learning styles (much like universal design makes public spaces and buildings accessible to people with all kinds of mobility, vision, and hearing needs). A lesson focused on universal design for learning principles is essentially an outline for creating flexible instructional goals, methods, materials, activities, and assessments that are accessible to everyone and that educators can customize. Inevitably, designing a lesson for those individuals who are in the margins benefits all students (Meyer & Rose, 2005).

Connell et al. (1997) define universal design as "products and environments to be usable by all people to the greatest extent possible without the need for adaptation or specialized design." Universal design reduces the need for adaptations. However, it is important to note that using universal design for learning principles in instruction does not automatically eliminate the need for adaptations. Some students may still require additional supports. Nevertheless, applying universal design concepts in lesson planning guarantees content access for the majority of students and lessens the need for extensive adaptations. For instance, designing online resources in a variety of accessible formats means no redevelopment if a student with a vision impairment joins the class. Indeed, following these principles in the initial planning stages will result in fewer time-consuming, ad hoc changes in the future.

CAST supports universal design for learning via three components: (1) representation, (2) action and expression, and (3) engagement (Meyer, Rose, & Gordon, 2014). *Adapting Unstoppable Learning* folds those components into systems thinking and applies them to the triangle of support. Specific learning tools facilitate universal design for learning activity planning (Castagnera et al., 2003).

Representation

The National Center on Universal Design for Learning advocates that, as they deliver lessons—or *represent* information—teachers use multiple means of representation to depict concepts and information that are necessary for student comprehension (CAST, 2011). For instance, this may mean modeling a mathematics problem in different ways and providing various solving methods, including textual, visual, and tactile representations with real-life examples, not only once but multiple times, throughout the lesson and unit. These modalities provide the accommodations students need. Delivering instructional input through creative representations ensures student access to quality curriculum.

Action and Expression

When planning for student input and output possibilities, educators must allow multiple means of intake and expression—text, images, sound, and video (CAST, 2011; Meyer & Rose, 2005). These accommodations apply to students' true physical actions and how they express their knowledge, such as how they interact with learning tools and how they reveal their understanding of learning targets. Accommodations promote choice; students can use their known abilities, strengths, and interests to arrive at and display the same learning outcome that others reach and reveal in other ways. The goal of encouraging these actions and expressions is to provide students opportunities to overcome barriers and facilitate an effective manner for them to demonstrate their growth and mastery of the learning target. *Scaffolding*, a form of differentiated instruction, provides students with graduated levels of support, allowing them opportunities for practice as they build fluency through action and expression (CAST, 2011).

Engagement

A teacher's goal is to maintain high levels of engagement as he or she delivers content and assessment activities. This third component of universal design for learning calls for educators to provide students with multiple means of engagement. Meyer and Rose (2005) explain that teachers create interest in the instruction they give through content organization, tools, adjusted challenge and support levels, rewards, incentives, and varied learning contexts. These accommodations help students sustain their motivation, which leads to sustained efforts and learning the executive function of self-regulation. Motivation itself is a scaffold of sorts, since without it students cannot sustain the efforts that learning requires (CAST, 2011).

Learning Tools

When planning a universal design for learning lesson, educators must focus on the what, why, and how of each activity. To help maintain that focus, Castagnera et al. (2003) provide three tools: (1) the student profile, (2) infused skills grid, and (3) academic unit lesson plan. Combining the three tools helps teachers further determine what curriculum adaptations they may need to provide in lesson delivery, tasks, and assessments, while still meeting the lesson's content objectives and standards. These tools also facilitate the determination of instructional and assistive technology, as well as personal supports. Rigor is maintained. In the section All Three Tools in Action (page 22), we'll take a look at how the three tools work together to support student success.

Educators can use the student profile, infused skills grid, and academic unit lesson plan to identify other students who may be struggling due to circumstances, such as language barriers, that interfere with learning. The aforementioned tools we present in this book all serve to better determine ways in which educators can adapt their instruction and activities; they are tools designed to build student capacity and aid in the learning process. Visit **go.SolutionTree.com/instruction** to access free reproducible versions of these tools for your own use.

Student Profile

The student profile addresses many important issues, including the student's strengths and interests; successful learning strategies, modifications, and accommodations; communication strategies; positive behavior support strategies; grading and assessment accommodations; and important health and family information. It is critical to note that a student profile also works for students who do not receive special education services but do require supports via other in-class interventions (such as MTSS or RTI[2]). A student's entire education team must be familiar with the student profile.

Student profiles accomplish the following.

- Help teachers get to know their students' individual needs (K. Elliot, personal communication, April 1, 2016)

- Inform lesson planning, instruction, and appropriate supports (D. Carlin, personal communication, April 1, 2016)

- Encourage teachers to focus on students' strengths and capabilities (B. Arnaiz, personal communication, April 1, 2016)

- Provide immediate start-of-year information about students with individualized education plans (IEPs) or language support needs (K. Elliot, personal communication, April 1, 2016)

- Allow teachers to create measurable academic and social learning objectives (K. Elliot, personal communication, April 1, 2016)

- Provide teachers with successful strategies and specific adaptations for individual students (A. Montferret, personal communication, March 30, 2016)

- Facilitate teachers feeling more comfortable and confident about how to teach students with varying needs (A. Montferret, personal communication, March 30, 2016)

An education team collaboratively creates the student profile by gathering information about a student through observations, family input, and feedback from others connected to the student's education plan. If a student receives special education services, information from the IEP is also included in the profile. The team, throughout the school year, updates areas of strength, successful learning strategies, and communication and behavior supports as they emerge. An IEP is a written document created for a student who is eligible for special education services; it outlines a student's educational supports and services. The team can create an all-encompassing student profile with information for all classes or subject areas. For instance, students can have one student profile that addresses important information for reading, writing, mathematics, science, social studies, and physical education. Student profiles best help meet a student's needs when all teachers have access to goals in all areas. That helps ensure that the student can continue working on these skills across the curriculum and across subjects. For example, it is important for a science teacher to understand her student's mathematics needs when she holds labs that involve formulas. Similarly, it would be imperative for English, history, and science teachers to know a student's reading and writing needs when making assignments that require students to cite evidence from a variety of sources.

The team shares the student profile with everyone who is developing the student's individual learning objectives and makes it readily accessible to all staff, including paraprofessionals and others who deliver and support instruction. (Chapter 4, page 59, talks about divvying up duties and plans for sharing information.) The student profile should be available in all planning meetings (for example, during IEP, student study team, and grade-level planning meetings) so people who are familiar with the student can contribute. Teachers are responsible for familiarizing themselves with the student profiles that others share with them, and they can review them as often as needed. Student profiles should always be up-to-date and consistently reviewed. For students receiving special education services, the profile should be revised shortly following an IEP meeting.

All teachers in *all* subjects should be aware of *all* the skills and goals the student is working on. This is especially important since generalization and independence are ultimate objectives. *Generalization* means students can apply a learned skill across a variety of settings as educators fade supports and students gain independence. To generalize a skill, a student may easily continue working on, for instance, a writing goal in mathematics and science, as well as a computation goal in English and social studies, if all teachers are aware of the need. For example, a student with a goal of learning to tell time can work on this skill in all classes if those teachers assign him or her to be the timekeeper during presentations and debates. Susana Jimenez, a high school paraprofessional who co-teaches and provides supports to students in a general education classroom, underscores that student profiles are particularly helpful when she is working with small groups because she can use them to confirm that students are working toward their goals (personal communication, April 13, 2016).

Eventually, the education team forwards the student profile to the next grade level, so that staff have a clear picture of how to best support the student.

Infused Skills Grid

The infused skills grid helps an education team determine how it will address a student's skills, needs, and expectations within each component of a course, subject, lesson, or unit. Teachers can also utilize this tool for students who do not receive special education services. The infused skills grid can help address targeted skill development to ensure that these skills are embedded throughout all students' daily schedules. The tool can help identify how to integrate a student's academic and functional goals and learning objectives within his or her daily schedule. Functional goals address nonacademic daily activities, such as organizing personal and school belongings, following a routine, or purchasing food during lunchtime.

Along the left side of the infused skills grid, an elementary teacher may list a student's schedule as shared reading, guided reading groups, mathematics, reading, art, music, lunch, and recess. It is important to include times between specific subject areas or classes, such as before and after school, breaks, recess, lunch, and so on. This is important because students can address many goals and objectives during these times. Then across the top of the grid the teacher lists the targeted skills the student is working on, such as comprehension, division, word problems, and arriving to class on time, generated from the student profile and family interviews. The education team considers and marks on the grid where and when the student can get additional instruction in those skills. It does not mean the student has to work on them every day during that time. A student's daily activities and needs are fluid and need to be flexible. However, students must have consistent opportunities to work on their goals.

If the education team completes the grid and a goal or skill still lacks a check mark throughout the day, the education team determines how the student can work on that goal or skill sometime within the current schedule. Sometimes it takes a little creativity. Sometimes the team changes a student's daily schedule, such as adding an activity during the day or making a switch in classes.

Infused skills grids accomplish the following (E. Castagnera, personal communication, February 28, 2017).

- Help teachers identify when they can address a student's skills, including academic and functional goals, as well as learning objectives, throughout the school day

- Inform the educational team if students are continuously working on skills and of any gaps in the schedule where important learning goals are not being addressed

- Provide teachers with a clear visual that students are having opportunities to work on skills and goals necessary for them to be successful in their general education classes

Academic Unit Lesson Plan

Not all instructional components may need adaptations, but teachers can plan those that do on the academic unit lesson plan. With the academic unit lesson plan, a student's education team determines whether the materials, instructional arrangements (including projects, supplemental activities, and homework), assessments, and final products are accessible to all students. The general educator shares his or her lesson plan on the left side of the form. In a collaborative discussion, the special education teacher and other involved personal supports (such as paraprofessionals, related service providers, and peers) determine what, if any, adaptations the current lesson plan needs. The academic unit lesson plan enables educators to strategically co-plan lessons, regardless of whether students receive special education services. This co-planning ensures a universally designed lesson plan.

Academic unit lesson plans accomplish the following (E. Castagnera, personal communication, February 28, 2017).

- Provide a tool with which educators can break down each lesson plan component and brainstorm in the areas of universal design and adapted learning

- Inform the educational team of specific detailed adaptations for each lesson plan component

- Encourage the collaborating team to maintain focus on the unit plan goals for the entire class, while simultaneously addressing individual students' needs

The student profile, infused skills grid, and academic unit lesson plan tools achieve the most when the entire education team creates and uses them in conjunction with each other. The following section shows how the team might accomplish that.

All Three Tools in Action

Using the universal design for learning tools to help assess and meet all student needs allows the education team to collaboratively establish the criteria necessary for each student's success. Teachers can shape learning objectives to define for students the expectations they must meet when they receive appropriate supports. Designing lessons and learning objectives that employ universal design for learning principles allows educators to determine clear expectations for student learning. The three tools together help educators create what John Hattie (2012) describes as:

> Good learning intentions, [which] are those that make clear to the students the type of mastery they need to attain, so that they understand where and when to invest energies, strategies, and thinking, and where they are positioned along the trajectory towards successful learning. (p. 47)

In addition to forming clear and accessible learning goals, systems thinking teachers focus on cultivating Unstoppable Learning principles, which thoroughly meld with universal design for learning components—specifically with the tools we have described: the student profile, infused skills grid, and academic unit lesson plan. For example, a focus on building communication and nurturing a supportive relationship leads educators to implement genuinely responsive strategies and approaches that establish sustainability. When teachers combine the universal design for learning framework with creating and collaborating on student profiles, they can attain a student-focused approach. This is when educators build relationships that allow them to truly understand students beyond a cumulative folder or an IEP. Then teachers and staff can begin to value the importance of designing a lesson with all student needs in mind.

Once they establish relationships with students and families, educators can begin to incorporate integral information about a student into their lesson planning via tools such as the student profile. More important, establishing genuine relationships with students allows team members to add meaningful information to a student profile. For instance, through conversations with a student's education team, teachers may realize the importance of working on various communication skills within the classroom. This would require everyone on a student's team—not just the speech-language pathologist—to directly and indirectly instruct about communication skills. Accordingly, a teacher could then aim to develop these foundational skills through daily instruction. In lesson design, this may take the shape of teaching students how to ask relevant questions, prompting them to elaborate on their responses, engaging in back-and-forth discussions, and facilitating all these skills through small-group and whole-class opportunities.

This type of information allows the education team to embed key information from the student profile and infused skills grid into an academic unit lesson plan. When doing so, educators purposefully design activities, projects, and assessments because they understand that one size does not fit all. Having said this, we also acknowledge that teachers may implement adaptations that they planned for individual students as strategies for all students or for a class as a whole, if it makes sense to do so.

The following exemplars of each tool are for a student who is an English learner (EL). That student, Stephanie, is an outgoing, inquisitive third grader who arrived at the school as a first grader. Stephanie is fluent in Spanish, her primary language, and also reads and writes in it. According to her student profile (figure 1.1, page 24), although Stephanie demonstrates effective decoding skills, her reading fluency and comprehension skills are at the first- and second-grade levels, respectively.

You can read in her student profile that Stephanie needs support in vocabulary development. Stephanie's writing is also an area of concern due to poor writing organization and difficulty expanding on her ideas. The general education teacher, along with her parents, EL instructor, and classroom paraprofessional, developed Stephanie's student profile by both prioritizing key areas of concern and brainstorming instructional strategies that have proved successful thus far. The team is able to glean important information from the family, such as daily home-life routines, languages spoken at home, and previous educational experiences.

Using this information, the education team used the infused skills grid (see figure 1.2, page 25) to determine when in Stephanie's daily schedule she could continuously work on practicing strategies to build her vocabulary, reading comprehension, descriptive writing, and other skills the team deemed important.

Student Profile

School name: Diversity Elementary   **Student name:** Stephanie Hernandez   **Room:** 12   **Age:** 8   **Grade:** 3
Daily schedule:

Shared reading—8:30–8:50   Lunch—12:00–12:35
Guided reading groups—8:55–9:55   Recess—12:35–12:50
Recess—10:00–10:15   Science or social studies—12:55–1:25
Writing—10:20–10:50   Physical education, library, and computer lab—1:30–2:00
Mathematics—10:55–11:55

Parent or guardian: Mr. and Mrs. Hernandez
Co-teachers: EL instructor—Mr. Linguals   **Classroom teacher**—Mrs. Koplanor   **Paraprofessional**—Ms. Sapport

Areas of strength, interest, and need:
Stephanie is an outgoing girl who loves sports and is very active. She enjoys cooking and going camping with her family. Stephanie enjoys volunteering answers and asking a lot of questions. She has been in the country for about two years. Her favorite subject is writing and she is good about expressing her opinions. She has difficulty with spelling, capitalization, writing organization, and expanding her ideas. Stephanie has great decoding skills and is able to sound out words she doesn't know. She applies the decoding rules she has learned most of the time. Her reading fluency is at a first-grade level; however, comprehension is at a second-grade level and she struggles with vocabulary. When Stephanie reads, she tends to rush. Stephanie loves going to the library and choosing picture books or magazines about sports, especially basketball and volleyball. Stephanie is skilled in single-, double-, and triple-digit addition and subtraction, but she is inconsistent with multiplication facts, which leads to challenges with division problems. Stephanie also has difficulty with word problems.

Successful learning strategies, modifications, or accommodations needed:
Stephanie benefits from chunked text, guided questioning, think-alouds, and pair sharing to increase her comprehension. Audio versions of text help her during independent reading opportunities to gain the key ideas from text. Having translated versions of text, one day prior, supports Stephanie so she participates more actively. Front-loading vocabulary, pairing concepts with multiple visuals, and highlighting cognates in Spanish help her comprehension. Supports such as a multiplication chart, calculator, picture representations, and manipulatives support her during mathematics instruction. Presenting key word problem information in list formats or graphics supports her ability to synthesize key information.

Communication strategies:
Stephanie is able to communicate her opinions well and ask questions when she does not understand what to do. Stephanie becomes very excited and will shout out answers. She often wants to be the first one to answer a question.

Positive behavior support strategies:
Stephanie enjoys chatting with others and sometimes requires reminders to stay focused. She is easily redirected by verbal prompting to attend to the task at hand. She also benefits from partnering with a student who is actively engaged in classroom activities.

Grading and assessment accommodations:
When Stephanie is assessed solely on her writing, her teacher and support staff will read and scaffold the reading assignment on which she bases her writing. Stephanie receives scaffolds and graphic organizers to structure her writing. When undergoing reading comprehension assessment, Stephanie receives access to audio text.

Important family and health information:
Stephanie primarily speaks Spanish at home. Stephanie enjoys translating for her parents when they go to doctors' appointments. She has been attending schools in this country since the age of six but did attend preschool and kindergarten in her home country.

Source: Adapted from Castagnera et al., 2003.

Figure 1.1: Sample student profile for student who is an English learner.

*Visit **go.SolutionTree.com/instruction** for a free reproducible version of this figure.*

Infused Skills Grid

School name: Diversity Elementary   **Student name:** Stephanie Hernandez   **Room:** 12   **Age:** 8   **Grade:** 3

Daily schedule:

Shared reading—8:30–8:50
Guided reading groups—8:55–9:55
Recess—10:00–10:15
Writing—10:20–10:50
Mathematics—10:55–11:55

Lunch—12:00–12:35
Recess—12:35–12:50
Science or social studies—12:55–1:25
Physical education, library, and computer lab—1:30–2:00

Parent or guardian: Mr. and Mrs. Hernandez

Co-teachers: EL instructor—Mr. Linguals   **Classroom teacher—**Mrs. Koplanor   **Paraprofessional—**Ms. Sapport

Activities, Subjects, Environments	Infused Skills							
	Comprehension	Vocabulary Development	Reading Fluency	Writing Organization	Descriptive Writing	Word Problems	Multiplication Facts	Division
Shared reading	X	X	X	X	X	X		
Guided reading groups	X	X	X	X	X	X		
Recess		X						
Writing	X	X	X	X	X	X	X	X
Mathematics	X	X			X	X	X	X
Lunch		X						
Recess		X						
Science and social studies	X	X	X	X	X	X	X	X
Physical education, library, and computer lab	X	X	X	X	X	X	X	X

Source: Adapted from Castagnera et al., 2003.

Figure 1.2: Sample infused skills grid for student who is an English learner.

*Visit **go.SolutionTree.com/instruction** for a free reproducible version of this figure.*

The infused skills grid enabled the team to see that Stephanie could consistently work on skills across content areas, library time, and even recess. For instance, it was apparent that she could address vocabulary development in *each* section of her day, including playtime. The classroom paraprofessional noted that Stephanie and her friends enjoyed playing Wall Ball every morning during recess. The game consists of teams of two players, where the serving player must hit the ball so that it bounces first on the ground and then against the wall; the receiving player must let the ball hit the wall and bounce once on the ground before taking his or her turn. The objective is to keep the pattern going of alternating bounces between the ground and the wall. The teams take turns competing to gain the most points before the ball bounces on the line or goes outside the boundaries. Stephanie's education team had the idea to randomly tape various vocabulary words all over the wall. The added challenge in this game of Wall Ball was that players had to try to touch as many vocabulary words as possible on the wall when they hit the ball. The players had to read the words aloud every time the ball touched one of the vocabulary cards. For bonus points, players stated whether the vocabulary word was an adjective, noun, verb, or adverb. This creative brainstorming session led the team to develop even more learning activities, which the teacher incorporated into physical education for the rest of the class.

Further, in the classroom, students engaged in descriptive writing activities during mathematics, social studies, and science. For example, the teacher presented Stephanie with a mathematics problem that showed each step worked out. Given a word bank with required vocabulary, a list of adjectives, and clearly outlined steps for solving the mathematics problem, Stephanie described, in writing, the process of solving the equation. To promote academic language practice, Stephanie read and verbally explained the process to a peer using the same resources. During the writing block where students chose their own topics, her teacher encouraged Stephanie to develop a descriptive mathematics story based on camping, which her student profile revealed she enjoys doing with her family. Parts of her writing requirements were to use specific sensory details to describe the campgrounds, each of her family members, the activities they did, and the foods they ate. To incorporate mathematics concepts, Stephanie discussed the amount of food that was divided by the number of family members who went camping and described how her family was grouped into teams to play a competitive game. Again, Stephanie received a list of adjectives pertinent to her topic, graphic organizers to structure her ideas, and sentence frames or sentence starters to assist her in elaborating on her thoughts. These activities incorporated a multitude of academic standards and supports and fueled her vocabulary development in a way that valued her interests and met her academic needs, which the infused skills grid documented.

Stephanie's language needs required specific types of strategies and supports. Hence, educators considered detailed adaptations during a science lesson on a butterfly's life cycle. The academic unit lesson plan in figure 1.3 shows an effective example with a plethora of hands-on activities and visuals; however, the column for possible adaptations on this lesson plan demonstrated how the plan further supported Stephanie's learning experience within specific lesson components. Although in this lesson design students fully engaged in observing, drawing, and building the butterfly's metamorphosis stages, some students still had difficulty formulating descriptive ways to relate their experiences. This discrepancy highlights the importance of differentiated instruction by providing scaffolds that some students, like Stephanie, may need to demonstrate their understanding of lesson content and objectives.

Academic Unit Lesson Plan				
School name: Diversity Elementary	**Subject:** Science	**Co-teachers:** **EL instructor**—Mr. Linguals **Classroom teacher**—Mrs. Koplanor **Paraprofessional**—Ms. Sapport		**Unit or lesson:** Life cycles
Major standards, objectives, and expectations for the lesson or unit: **Content objectives—** Students will be able to identify and sequence the stages of metamorphosis. **Language objectives—** Students will be able to verbally explain the similarities and differences in the stages. **Social objectives—** Students will work in cooperative pairs to analyze the stages of metamorphosis.				

Materials—books, media, worksheets, software, and so on:
 	
• Metamorphosis stages visual, vocabulary graphic organizer, concept map, prediction chart
 	
• *The Very Hungry Caterpillar* book
 	
• Monarch caterpillar, egg, chrysalis, butterfly aquarium, paper, cotton, toothpicks, crayons, shoe box
		Adaptations:
		
		• Reformat graphic organizers to contain key words
		
		• Provide sentence frames for prediction chart
		
		  • I predict _____ will _____ because _____.
		
		  • Since _____ my prediction is _____.		

Figure 1.3: Sample academic unit lesson for student who is an English learner.   continued →

Instructional arrangements: Is there time and opportunity for large, group, and co-op group learning centers, individual activities, or nonclassroom instruction? Does it change daily? Explain.	Adaptations:

• Whole-class instruction
  • Front loading: Vocabulary graphic organizer
  • Shared reading: *The Very Hungry Caterpillar*
  • Visual: Analyze each stage of metamorphosis
• Learning centers (pairs rotate)
  • Observation station (aquarium with egg, caterpillar, and so on)
  • Sequencing station
  • Diorama station
• Individual activity
  • Descriptive paragraphs
	• Verbal modeling and practice to explain each stage at each station
	• Sentence starters and frames for written response or verbal response
	  • I observe that _____.
	  • First _____ happened, then _____.
	• Word banks

Projects, supplemental activities, and homework:
 	
Concept map—Brainstorm specific details about each stage using their observation sketches, sequencing graphic organizer, and diorama.
 	
Prediction chart— Write and draw a picture in each box showing where, how, and why; students will briefly explain where the butterfly will go, how the butterfly will get there, and why the butterfly chose to go there.
	Adaptations:
	• Sample concept maps featuring other cycles
	• Peer support to point out and discuss key components
	• Sentence starters—
	  • I predict the butterfly will . . .
	  • The butterfly will get there by . . .
	  • I believe this because . . .

Assessments and final products: Summarize actual student performance on the reverse. Attach examples as appropriate. Using the lesson vocabulary and descriptive words, write one or two paragraphs explaining what happens in each stage and a brief prediction of where the butterfly will go.	Adaptations: • Sequencing sentence starters • Word bank and visuals with adjectives • Verbal response instead of written response

Source: Adapted from Castagnera et al., 2003.

*Visit **go.SolutionTree.com/instruction** for a free reproducible version of this figure.*

These three exemplars demonstrate how teachers can use these tools for the benefit of any student or group of students who needs additional academic supports.

The Takeaways

The concepts we explore in this chapter—Unstoppable Learning, the triangle of support, and universal design for learning—help make education accessible. With the help of the student profile, infused skills grid, and academic unit lesson tools, educators can determine and communicate the specific needs students have for learning adaptations. Systems thinking teachers maintain student-focused classrooms by using the principles of relationships, communication, responsiveness, and sustainability. The triangle of support allows educators to familiarize themselves with the variety of adaptations that may facilitate student learning in any lesson or activity. The universal design for learning framework complements this by helping teachers forecast learning barriers and implement solutions through the use of flexible lesson arrangements.

CHAPTER 2

MAKING ACCOMMODATIONS AND MODIFICATIONS WHILE ENSURING RIGOR

All students must have access to the general education curriculum. Adaptations ensure that is possible. A variety of useful, creative strategies provide accommodations and modifications from which many students benefit. While adaptations are ultimately individualized, some general approaches can be useful. This chapter explains those approaches and fleshes out the adaptations that Fisher and Frey (2015) introduced in *Unstoppable Learning*. Figure 2.1 shows the array of options educators should consider when providing adaptations.

Figure 2.1: Adaptation types.

We remind education teams of two things: (1) that differentiated instruction through the use of accommodations, modifications, and accelerated learning falls under the umbrella of adaptations, and (2) to remain mindful of curriculum standards, including when and how they change depending on student needs. Many strategies and supports fall within these categories and often overlap. Does a student require more rigor by increasing difficulty or complexity, and if so, how does this change compare to the standards this task represents? The *difficulty* measures the amount of effort the student must exert to complete the task. The *complexity* signals the amount of thinking, action, or knowledge the student must employ to complete the task.

Asking these driving questions will help educators choose which type of adaptation to use.

- What is the objective of this particular task for this specific student?

- What aspects of the task do I need to adapt in order to differentiate instruction and how will I accomplish this?

- What accommodations should I consider prior to modifications?

- For students who are meeting the standards required for a diploma, will this adaptation affect the standard?

- Are these adaptations going to be effective and meaningful?

- Are these adaptations age and grade-level appropriate?

Adapting learning tasks and assessments may seem daunting. However, as teachers learn to collaborate with students' education teams and families and familiarize themselves with the variety of learning styles and available adaptations, they will see their curriculum, lesson design, and instruction improve. In essence, teachers will build an archive of knowledge, tools, strategies, and adapted lesson plans that will foster the growth of all students. Over time, as collaboration increases and adaptations become second nature, educators will automatically implement these adaptations as strategies and tools that become best practices because they improve the whole lesson and provide access to all students. Even though some think adaptations are only needed for students with disabilities, in truth, any student may gain from adaptations at any given time. This includes gifted students in accelerated learning programs and twice-exceptional students, who are gifted and have a disability, as well as any student in the class who may need extra support for a given lesson. Ultimately, all students benefit from accessibility.

Teachers should challenge students and constantly consider how to reduce the adaptations they receive as they become more successful and independent in class. For example, when fourth grader Brooke received vocabulary assessments with her peers in class, the teacher reduced the number of vocabulary words from ten to five.

Halfway through the year, the teacher realized she was still only giving Brooke five vocabulary words—even though she had successfully completed all five for several weeks. The teacher realized she should try giving Brooke six words. By the end of the year, Brooke was up to eight vocabulary words a week.

And finally, all students benefit from high expectations from their teachers. This chapter explains how educators can maintain rigor as they provide adaptations through accommodations and modifications.

Accommodations

Accommodations affect how students access and express their understanding of the content. Again, this form of support does not alter the instructional level, content, or standards criteria. Teachers often consider accommodations for students with mild learning, behavioral, emotional, or speech difficulties, but they also serve students who have giftedness and twice-exceptionality. It is critical that accommodations are viewed as supports that maintain rigor rather than an adaptation that reduces it. Teachers may implement curriculum accommodations or modifications, depending on whether the extent of the adaptation changes the standards. These include same, only less; streamlined curriculum; same activity with infused objective; and curriculum overlapping (explained more in detail on page 47). This section focuses on adaptions that do not change the standard, therefore referred to as *accommodations*. Educators provide accommodations in the areas of curriculum, technology, and the environment, all three of which are discussed in the following sections. This section also addresses gifted and twice-exceptional students and assessment accommodations.

Curriculum Accommodations

Curriculum accommodations address how teachers present information to a student, as well as how he or she demonstrates competency. For example, eighth grader LaRon struggles with written expression and the ability to write coherently. When he receives the opportunity to orally provide answers, rather than writing them, he is successful.

When a teacher notices that a student is struggling, he or she might first provide support in the form of tutoring. Some students benefit from scaffolding provided by personal supports within the classroom. This includes different levels of prompting such as guided questions, hints, and brief explanations. (Chapter 3, page 53, talks about personal supports.) If that isn't sufficient to enable the student to master learning targets, he or she must then consider other accommodations. Again, driving questions guide this process. What is the task's objective? With what part of the task does the student struggle? Through observation and work samples, educators identify where in the learning process the student requires additional support. If the student is working toward a high school diploma, will the proposed accommodation change the required standards, putting the student's graduation in jeopardy? If this is the case, and the student's progress is not improving despite accommodations, the educational team must collaborate to identify the reasons why. If an educator determines that a student requires modifications that alter the standards, the IEP team must make the decision.

Depending on the student, he or she may need to initially attempt a learning task with very little, if any, accommodation. That allows educators to assess the student's ability level, and it promotes problem-solving skills because it allows the student to engage in healthy and carefully monitored struggle. Teachers, and even students themselves, can be pleasantly surprised to discover emerging capacities and new thresholds. It is important to be mindful of such possibilities and avoid automatically supplying an adaptation simply because it always has been.

Keeping this in mind, educators should encourage communication with students so they advocate for themselves—asking for support, but also revealing when the supports begin making assignments too easy. For instance, six months into the school year, a student we know, who had regularly requested accommodated assessments, self-advocated to let his biology teacher know that the latest exam on ecology and evolution was "pretty easy" and that he was ready for a version without adaptations. Moreover, achieving independence is the ultimate goal for students. Therefore, allowing adaptations to fade is always the aim. Notably, as students become proficient, they develop a fortified infrastructure of increased knowledge and skill that will serve them during more difficult assignments.

Teachers can also individualize accommodations based on needs, learning styles, and interests. The types of adaptations that will work best for a particular student are not always evident, nor can an educator presume exactly how a change in the curriculum, instructional presentation, or classroom setting might benefit a student. Strong relationships with the student, family, and other educators, along with a detailed student profile and infused skills grid, facilitate this process. No matter the case, adapting instruction and tasks means that the teacher considers all parts of the curriculum, including the content, methodology, and delivery.

Consider universal design for learning when designing classroom instruction and implementing scaffolds for background knowledge building. It will naturally provide accommodations to those students who need it. For example, Linda Tilton (2001) shares the following tips that teachers can easily incorporate for adapting curriculum.

- Make directions concise and easy to understand.
- Follow all key terms or vocabulary words with examples.
- Be conscientious of the way you lay out materials. For instance, when designing an activity on paper, avoid overcrowding. Paper assignments tend to have a variety of activities on one page, such as open-ended questions,

graphs, and matching key terms to the definition. This can be confusing and overwhelming for some students. Instead, reduce the number of different activities on a single page.

- Avoid double-sided papers. Flipping the page can be difficult when answering questions about a passage on another page. It is much easier for a student to have two separate pieces of paper side by side.

- Allow adequate white space to benefit students who write large letters. When students do not receive enough space to write, they may not completely answer the question. This is important for any student with fine motor difficulty, and can benefit elementary students who are learning to write.

When educators have determined that a student needs accommodations, they should consider the task's reading level and length. Depending on the student and his or her independent reading level (determined by formal and informal reading assessments), a variety of options make reading material accessible. For instance, a student can access a text that is not at his or her reading level through purchased audio books or digital print utilizing text-to-speech applications. Another option is to provide the student with a summary of the key points to enable comprehension and provide access to the targeted content. Some students may find listening and writing at the same time difficult. Consider any number of options, including providing notes prior to classroom discussions, creating an outline or graphic organizer to visually support note taking during class, and assigning note takers and posting those notes on the class website to also benefit students who have chronic absences. In addition to notes, teachers can post online audio recordings of classroom instruction, which allows students with Internet access to review it later.

Table 2.1 (page 36) lists some accommodations that address both student input (how students receive information) and output (how students show what they have learned). It includes technology, which we explain in this chapter's next section.

Technological Supports

Teachers *make* accommodations, but *provide* technological support, as evidenced in the triangle of support (Castagnera et al., 2003). Because of rapid technological advances and the high demand for competence from new software and devices, many more students may require supports. As a tradeoff, technology can make assignments, projects, and assessments more accessible, while also increasing student engagement and participation. Susana Jimenez, a high school paraprofessional, highlights how technology has provided access to an exclusively Spanish-speaking student who joined the ninth-grade classes she supports (personal communication, April 13, 2016). The student's computer translates words to English for her. The access was made even more thorough when teachers embedded accommodations into this student's individual private page on a class website as part of the school's learning management system.

Table 2.1: Meaningful Accommodations

Input	Output

• Alternate formats:
   • Audio text
   • Braille
   • Large print
   • Oral or signed administration of directions, assignments, and texts
   • Amplified or projected texts
• Alternate support aids:
   • Dictionary or glossary
   • Multiplication or division charts
   • Customizable graphic organizers and maps
• Altered time aids:
   • Additional time
   • Preteaching
   • Interim check-ins
   • Organizational aids
	• Altered volume aids:
	   • Fewer items to complete
	   • Chunked larger tasks
	• Transcription and scribing:
	   • Student dictates answers to a scribe, who bubbles onto a Scantron sheet
	   • Student records spoken or signed language, and another student transcribes recording into written form

Source: Adapted from Fisher & Frey, 2015.

Computer programs and devices provide support so students can accomplish tasks, and assistive technology increases students' independence. However, while technology may provide accessibility, it does not necessarily provide usability. *Accessibility* is something that all individuals with a variety of needs can easily use, whereas *usability* is the technology's effectiveness and efficiency. Providing technology alone is not enough. It is critical that educators determine whether the technology is accessible *and* usable.

Technological supports range from high tech (such as computer software) to low tech (such as smaller tools like highlighter pens). Trent's accommodation is a low-tech example. Sometimes, the amount of information presented at one time can be difficult for students. When Trent, a seventh grader, is assigned numerous mathematics problems, the sight of so many problems at once overwhelms him. He shuts down and does not attempt any problems. His teacher takes a manila envelope and cuts out the bottom and a large rectangular window on one side, then places the mathematics sheet with problems inside in such a way that Trent can see only one row of problems at a time through the rectangle. Decreasing the number of problems he can see reduces his anxiety and allows him to focus.

The following sections explain the kinds of technological supports, from low-tech tools and computer software to specific websites, you might provide to a student.

Tools and Software

Teachers can meet students' needs with the help of tools that provide fine and gross motor or hearing support, as well as with computer software. Conversely, teachers must sometimes adapt technology, such as the Internet, for student accessibility. Table 2.2 lists various technological supports that allow accommodations.

Table 2.2: Technology Supports

Technology Support	How This Technology Provides Support
Fine and Gross Motor Supports	
Pencil grips	Supports grasp when writing
Slant boards	Assists with posture, wrist extension, vision strain
Raised-line paper	Provides a sensory guide to aid in legibility
Sensory seat cushion	Improves posture and provides sensory input
Educational Aids	
Concept maps	Creates visual support for comprehension
Talking calculator	Provides audio support
Spelling and grammar checks	Proofreads text to reduce the chance of errors
Reading guides	Highlights one line of text at a time
Magnifiers	Enlarges font for students with visual impairments
Timers	Encourages time management
Communication Tools	
Audio recordings	Aids comprehension
Braille	Provides access for students who have visual impairments
Speech output devices	Facilitates communication
FM listening devices	Provides access for students who are deaf and hard of hearing
Computer Adaptations	
Alternate keyboards and mice	Provides physical support, reduces input choices, aids comprehension via color and graphics
Text-to-speech software	Aids comprehension
Speech-to-text software	Physically supports the mechanics of writing
Concept map	Aids the writing process using graphic organizers; view Draft:Builder at http://donjohnston.com/draftbuilder
Word-prediction software	Aids the writing process; Co:Writer (http://donjohnston.com/cowriter) works with Google Chrome

continued →

Technology Support	How This Technology Provides Support
Computer Adaptations	
Digital audio recorder pen with embedded camera	Allows electronic upload of handwritten and aural notes that appear in original handwritten format or typed; Livescribe Smartpen is an example of this technology
Screen-reading programs	Grants access to students who have visual impairments
Variable speed recorders	Aids in comprehension by controlling audio speed
Screen recording	Provides audio support paired with visuals onscreen; view Screencastify at www.screencastify.com
Movie recording	Allows students to provide their answers via video recording; view Flipgrid at www.flipgrid.com

For example, a twelfth grader named Caleb uses speech recognition software so he can speak his words into his computer. The software converts his speech to text so he can complete written work. This helps him meet deadlines, because it takes him a long time to type. He uses the software for both academic and personal tasks.

Websites

Many schools use classroom or teacher websites. These should be accessible to all students. Web Accessibility in Mind (WebAIM) is an organization that offers services and resources for designing accessible online experiences for all users, with special consideration for people with varying accessibility differences. WebAIM (2013) asserts that a perceivable website takes into account the three primary senses: (1) sight, (2) hearing, and (3) touch. Additionally, an accessible website alters information from one form into another, such as transforming text into audio or Braille via various assistive technology devices. Its navigation is consistent, predictable, and clearly labeled.

Furthermore, an accessible website considers the following (WebAIM, 2013).

- Not everyone uses a standard keyboard and mouse to navigate his or her computer due to physical or visual disabilities. While some utilize a roller ball in lieu of a mouse, others may use a mouth stick to rely on keyboard functionality. Consider various input methods such as mouse-dependent versus keyboard-dependent access points.

- Interaction methods such as navigation tools like an index, site maps, and site search help students quickly find information, thereby allowing them to bypass irrelevant or extraneous pieces of content.

- Timing limits such as user-controlled versus preset timers allow students to have extended time.

- Error recovery such as confirmation screens, error alerts, and warnings notifies all students, providing them a second chance to recover from a mistake (such as clicking the wrong link) or confirm their choice.

Programs such as Pocket (https://getpocket.com) allow users to create a clean, ad-free view of the website on a computer, smartphone, or tablet at no cost to the consumer. Read&Write for Google Chrome is an app that increases accessibility to documents in Google Drive by providing tools such as a picture dictionary, word predictions, simplified text, and easily followed text-to-speech, dual-color highlighting.

Environmental Accommodations

Sometimes environmental accommodations are necessary. For example, a sixth grader named Tara struggles with participating in classroom tasks, which has become evident in her daily progress. As a result of teachers collaborating with her speech-language pathologist and audiologist, and speaking with Tara herself, it has become clear she would benefit from being seated in the front corner of the classroom. She wears hearing aids and glasses. Therefore, being close to the teacher and to the projection screen makes it easier for her to hear and see important information. When her seating changes, her progress immediately improves.

Distractions can be troublesome. Consider adjusting a seat or work area away from high-traffic areas, classroom speakers, heating or air units, and windows. While selectivity is important, do not consistently group the same students together in assigned seating nor assigned pairing or grouping. All students will benefit from sitting next to and working with a variety of peers.

Be mindful of classroom lighting. Asem Obeidat and Raed Al-Share (2012) find that of all the essential environmental features—noise, glare, air quality, temperature, seat comfort and arrangement—lighting was the most important in creating a conducive learning environment. Unfortunately, lighting can cause headaches and eyestrain due to the hum and flicker of fluorescent lighting and glare of fluorescent lighting, daylight, window blinds, and projection screens (Winterbottom & Wilkins, 2009). In a study about cognitive reactions to fluorescent lighting, Igor Knez (2014) deduces that "subjects felt less enthusiastic, elated, excited, euphoric, lively, peppy and less relaxed, content, at rest, calm, serene, at ease," despite the flickering being visually imperceptible. Classrooms with proper lighting create an environment that increases concentration and cognitive performance in students.

Choose colors that adorn and enhance classrooms. Kristi S. Gaines and Zane D. Curry (2011) present research that supports the notion that color indeed does affect student attention, behavior, and achievement. It is important to note that too much color can be just as damaging as not enough. Overstimulating colors create sensory overload, whereas not enough color in classrooms can be stressful and nonproductive. Several sources suggest subdued warm neutrals, especially for students with autism, such as pastels, neutral beiges, and browns (Myler, Fantacone, & Merritt, 2003; Stokes, n.d.).

Consider providing students with larger, clearer work areas that are free from unneeded materials. For some students, teachers should strategically manage and organize the volume of classroom sounds, transition times, and breaks. Teachers may need to provide specific times for students to organize their belongings. All of these environmental accommodations have the potential to support all students.

Accommodations for Students With Giftedness and Twice-Exceptionality

Students who have giftedness—whether they're gifted alone or gifted as well as having a disability (also referred to as *twice-exceptional*)—also require and benefit from a variety of curriculum adaptations. Further, it is wise to note that a student with giftedness may not be gifted in all areas.

Accelerated learning for students requires differentiated instruction. Educators are cautioned not to fall into the routine of solely increasing the workload (VanTassel-Baska & Stambaugh, 2005). This redundancy may result in stifled learning. Determining the depth and pace of learning guides teachers who are making instructional decisions. Educators accomplish this differentiation in various ways, including compacted curriculum as well as extension and enrichment activities. Fisher and Frey (2015) advocate that *compacting* the curriculum allows students to move quickly through the areas they have already mastered. With compacting, they gain access to new content that enhances their knowledge acquisition. Incorporating *extension activities* increases the depth of the content they can cover (Fisher & Frey, 2015). Extension activities increase the depth to which students study content. For instance, a lesson on water pollution in biology class may require students to identify the specific chemicals in contaminated water and produce a lab report. As an extension activity, students could design a public service announcement encouraging their community to reduce water pollutants. This assignment could be a collaborative effort among students who could then go on to share their presentation, video, or debate in a community area of their choice, allowing for more enrichment. *Enrichment activities* require that educators assess students in their areas of interest and then provide meaningful, engaging activities centered on those interests.

Students with giftedness should have consistent contact with teachers. If students are able to complete work independently and do not regularly need teacher engagement, purposeful communication is necessary so the teacher can re-evaluate meaningful activities that have sufficient depth and complexity (VanTassel-Baska & Stambaugh, 2005). Additionally, all students need teacher support and instruction throughout the process.

Students who are considered twice-exceptional display an area of giftedness as well as a disability, such as a specific learning disability or autism. The National Association for Gifted Children (NAGC, n.d.) warns that students who are twice-exceptional are hard to identify because they comprehend a curriculum that fits a general classroom. Administering "a comprehensive evaluation that includes a cognitive ability test . . . and [learning] as much information as possible about a student's cognitive and academic profiles, as well as information about the student's social-emotional and behavioral presentation" helps teachers identify these easily missed students (Assouline, Foley Nicpon, & Whiteman, 2010 as cited in NAGC, n.d., pp. 2–3). Educators who are familiar specifically with giftedness and counselors who make diagnoses are a good resource as well (NAGC, n.d.).

Cherylynn Moody (2014) finds that one of the most effective strategies for twice-exceptional students in general education classrooms is to assess students' strengths and weaknesses to determine how to adapt the curriculum for these students. Expert panels from Moody's (2014) research recommend teaching advanced and higher-level thinking models while embedding necessary adaptations. An example would be to create extension activities as part of a current lesson being taught while also providing any needed adaptations such as speech-to-text applications and audiobooks paired with highlighting of text while the student reads.

Assessment Accommodations

When teachers adapt classroom assessments in addition to curriculum, this allows students to more accurately demonstrate what they know. Otherwise, the assessments for students needing accommodations will be inaccurate. The adapted assessment approach begins with determining what to assess and how to do it.

To collect accurate progress data on all students, especially for students with disabilities, it is critical that educators reduce assessments' standard error of measurement. All assessments will have data that are not 100 percent accurate—an error of measurement. The smaller the standard error of measurement, the more accurate the test results. If students incorrectly answer questions because they misunderstand them, feel overwhelmed by their appearance, or get confused by the format, then assessment will not yield accurate results.

Educators can reduce the standard error of measurement by allowing students to provide alternate formats, such as projects, oral presentations, and a variety of written assignments. For example, Hannah, a tenth grader enrolled in world history, has a good understanding of the content her essay question addresses. After completing her essay, Hannah feels frustrated and discouraged. Part of the essay prompt asked, "What were some consequences of World War II?" She does not know the meaning of the word *consequence*. When the prompt asks instead, "What happened because of World War II?" she skillfully responds to the prompt and accurately demonstrates her mastery.

Always consider making accommodations such as defining vocabulary in parentheses next to the academic word you want students to understand or providing a sample response or word bank to support students' knowledge of the topic prior to modifying any assessment. If accommodations are not enough support, exploring a variety of modifications is the next step.

In these next several sections, we describe variations for the following assessment types: multiple choice, true or false, fill in the blank, matching, and essays. Parallel problems, mathematics frames, and study guides are also solutions worth investigating.

Multiple Choice

Tilton (2001) highlights several changes teachers can make to multiple-choice questions. In addition to offering fewer answer choices, arrange answers vertically instead of horizontally. Figure 2.2 shows arrangements. These changes increase readability. Some students get confused when choices run into each other horizontally.

Nonexample with horizontal answers

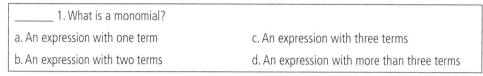

Example with adapted vertical answers

Figure 2.2: Nonexample and example of multiple-choice arrangement.

Always provide a complete question-and-answer set on a page before beginning a new page. The bold text in figure 2.3 shows the nonexample of splitting a question-and-answer set.

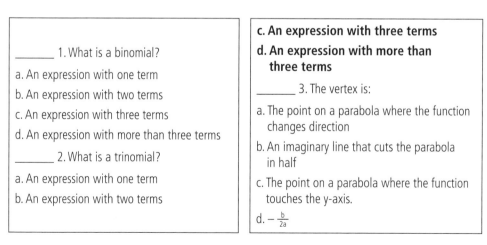

Source: © 2016 Arturo Cuevas, Health Sciences High and Middle College. Used with permission.

Figure 2.3: Nonexample of question and answer spanning pages.

True or False

True or false questions must be both precise and clear, containing clear directions and only one fact (Tilton, 2001). When two facts appear in one sentence, with one being true and the other false, it can confuse students. Are students supposed to write *yes* or *no*, *Y* or *N*, *true* or *false*, or *T* or *F*? Do they circle the letters *T* or *F*? If so, what do those letters represent? See figure 2.4.

Nonexample	Example
Directions: Answer the following T/F questions. 1.T/F: The Gulf War began in 1990 and was also known as Operation Desert Shield.	Directions: Circle True if the sentence is correct. Circle False if the sentence is incorrect. 1.The Gulf War began in 1990. True or False 2. The Gulf War was also known as Operation Desert Shield. True or False

Figure 2.4: Nonexample and example of true or false question.

Fill in the Blank

Provide word banks for fill-in-the-blank questions. Provide only one blank per question and ensure it is large enough for an answer from someone with poor fine motor control. Questions should be specific (Tilton, 2001). For example, "An elephant is a _____ animal" could be answered with the following words: *big*, *large*, or *gray*. If the teacher is inquiring for the answer of *mammal*, the question should be, "The class of animal that an elephant belongs to is _____." If necessary, convert fill-in-the-blank questions into direct questions such as, "What class of animal is an elephant?"

Matching

Tilton (2001) suggests improving matching questions by providing the definitions or longer answers on the left side of the page. This way, students first read the left column, which has a longer phrase. They are able to then scan the right column, since it consists of short words or phrases. It is much easier to scan a column of words or short phrases than it is to read longer, more cumbersome phrases. Also, avoid including more than ten matching pairs. An equal number of items to match can reduce student confusion. And, as always, clear directions are essential. Should students draw lines between pairs or write the corresponding letter on the corresponding blank space? Figure 2.5 (page 44) shows an example of an accessible matching assessment. Limit choices to one word or short phrases, and always provide a complete question-and-answer set on a page before beginning a new page. You can see that only five pairs appear on each page of the text. The bold line indicates a new page.

Directions: Draw a line between each state and its matching capital.

California	Phoenix
Washington	Sacramento
Oregon	Carson City
Nevada	Salem
Arizona	Olympia

Directions: Write the letter of each capital next to the state.

California ____	a. Phoenix
Washington ____	b. Sacramento
Oregon ____	c. Carson City
Nevada ____	d. Salem
Arizona ____	e. Olympia

Matching

Match each item in column A with an item in column B.

Write the correct letters on the blank spaces.

____ 1. A person, place, thing, or idea	a. determiner
____ 2. A word that limits a noun	b. adverb
____ 3. A word that describes a verb	c. noun
____ 4. A word that describes a noun	d. interjection
____ 5. A short exclamation found within a sentence	e. adjective

1

____ 6. An appeal to credibility; an expert is involved; a set of shared values	f. linear plot structure
	g. ethos
____ 7. An appeal to logic	h. pathos
____ 8. An appeal to emotion	i. logos
____ 9. Follows a logical order or sequence; its sequence is beginning–middle–end	j. non-linear plot structure
____ 10. Is unpredictable; its sequence jumps around in time	

2

Figure 2.5: Examples of matching.

Essays

Students may share their essays orally with their teachers or record their voices in place of writing their words. Also, knowing potential questions ahead of time allows students to plan and reduces their anxiety. For example, three students in the same class were provided with varying levels of support to complete the same assignment. Francisco, an eighth grader, while unable to write or type easily, can compose a thoughtful response to his English class essay prompt with supporting claims by sharing it orally with the teacher. Irina dictates her essay to a peer who types it. Both students receive additional time on the assigned task. Other students receive graphic organizers and outlines. In addition, the teacher modifies an essay assignment about *Romeo and Juliet* for Ava asking her instead to create a pictorial collage representing love and hate.

Parallel Problems

Parallel problems allow the student to receive assessment of his or her ability to complete a mathematics problem using an identical example as a guide. Parallel problems are example problems that have been completed by the teacher and show all or some of the steps needed to solve the problem. The parallels allow students to see exactly what teachers ask of them. This supports students who may take insufficient or illegible notes. Teachers can base the extent to which they solve the parallel problem on the level of support the student requires. If they just need a jump-start, the example may contain just the first few steps. If a student requires visual support, then the teacher may provide every step or guiding steps such as *Circle like terms, Combine like terms*, or *Divide*.

Mathematics Frames

Teachers would not assess the student on his or her ability to recall the steps. If students are successful with parallel problems, eventually educators can fade to only providing *mathematics frames*, which is an equation missing the numbers. Simple, direct written steps such as *Add all the coins together* can ensure the student understands how to use the mathematics frame. Figure 2.6 is a mathematics frame example.

Figure 2.6: Sample mathematics frame.

Study Guides

It is worth mentioning that some students have difficulty knowing what and how to study. Supports can come in a variety of ways, including modeling and prompting. Completed visual study guides or guides designed for students to complete themselves can be useful. Study guides include the key content points and terms that students should know for an upcoming assignment, project, or assessment. If students complete the study guides themselves, a staff member should check accuracy.

What Actions Do I Need to Take Based on the Student Assessment Data?

Continual assessment and progress monitoring are integral. If student assessment data demonstrate lack of progress, ask a few questions: Does the assessment allow for a true and appropriate measure of student competency or growth? If teachers are unsure of the answer, did they incorporate applicable assessment strategies according to the individual student's learning objective and expectations?

Determining whether an assessment is an authentic representation of a student's present mastery level relies heavily on an education team's ability to follow through on previously established student success criteria. If teachers deem students to have shown genuine areas of concern based on the given assessment, then they should consider using this information to revise instructional delivery methods. That being said, teachers should hold students accountable to their individualized goals and specific learning objectives when the team determines growth or mastery. Keep growth in mind and don't penalize students when they do not immediately demonstrate mastery. Acknowledging that a student is continually gaining and developing skills throughout the learning process is as important as mastery. Regardless of the demonstrated growth, measure student gains in comparison to the individual student, not to the rest of the class.

Modifications

Some students continue to struggle despite accommodations. Those students may then require modifications to the learning objectives or activities that alter what the teacher expects the student to learn and produce. If a student's progress is not improving despite accommodations, the educational team collaborates to identify why. It must be a collaborative IEP team decision if a student requires modifications. Educators can employ useful, simple strategies to implement modifications when they are designing curriculum. Students may be mastering only a portion of the content standards. Therefore, teachers most often consider modifications for students with more significant learning differences.

As with accommodations, it is critical to remember that not every assignment, assessment, or activity may need modification. Even though students receive extensive modified content, they should still learn and participate in the same subject area as the rest of the class.

Modifications are not an effort to make the curriculum easier; rather, they distill what the teacher wants this particular student to learn from a specific assignment or activity. Prior to making modifications, the teacher—in collaboration with the education team—should know what the objective is for both the assignment and the individual student, taking into consideration all of the student's needs, learning abilities, and IEP goals. If applicable, the student's objective will be different from the original assignment. However, the student is still demonstrating competence in the *same content area*. For example, most students in Reym's class receive the objective of writing a five-paragraph essay comparing and contrasting two readings. Reym, however, requires a modification, and so he will come up with two lists to accomplish the same objective. If and when a student is ready to move away from modifications, you can scaffold with accommodations.

Adaptations as Accommodations or Modifications

In *Unstoppable Learning*, Fisher and Frey (2015) advocate for these modifications: (1) same, only less, (2) streamlining curriculum, (3) same activity with infused objectives, and (4) curriculum overlapping. These four adaptations can function as either accommodations or modifications, depending on the extent to which teachers provide the adaptations.

Though these approaches are described as modifications, any of these approaches implemented to an extent that does not alter the standards could be implemented as an accommodation. It's always important to remember that while you can adapt instruction numerous ways, the focus should always remain on what a particular student should gain from an activity, while being mindful of standards. However, as mentioned, some students will require modifications that may include assignment and assessment changes.

Same, Only Less

This approach provides the same task, but less of it. If a task proves too long for a student, reduce the task without altering the questions, vocabulary, or content. For example, if teachers ask students to work in groups, with each individual sharing ten vocabulary words, certain students could share five key vocabulary words instead. If students are completing a thirty-question classroom assessment, give only twenty questions. If teachers assign eight mathematics questions to the class, assign five questions instead to those who require the adaptation. If assigning a five-page essay, reduce it to a three-page essay. If the student still cannot successfully complete the task, his or her teacher can reduce the same assignment much more substantially, making those alterations if a student requires that level of support. For example, teachers could change the five-page essay to a pictorial storybook based on the same prompt or topic that describes each picture with one or two sentences.

Streamlined Curriculum

This approach abbreviates the content. The amount of information teachers provide can overwhelm some students. In that case, it makes sense to streamline the curriculum. For example, if students are reading a novel, then the teacher can help them access the content by providing a summary or shortened version that addresses the key components. This allows students the opportunity to focus solely on the content they need to address. Include the plot points and characters that are critical to understanding the novel's meaning and from the corresponding class activities. Provide summaries, outlines, and graphic organizers that give students the pertinent information.

For some students, sifting through information and extracting the essential components can be extremely difficult. A modification in language arts can come in the form of requiring a list of main points instead of an essay. Simplify vocabulary for a science unit on cells by focusing only on key points of these definitions. Tilton (2001) advocates that "It is helpful to differentiate between *must know* and *nice to know* material; not every assignment falls into the must know category for every student" (p. xx).

Same Activity With Infused Objective

This approach provides the same activity but also includes an objective that a student is working on. Some students have a variety of IEP goals and objectives to focus on and that they strive to meet daily. In these cases, teachers can incorporate such goals into daily classroom assignments, activities, and projects. For example, if a student is working on answering questions in complete sentences, then the teacher can integrate this opportunity during all class activities by creating prewritten questions and a place to answer these types of questions within the same activity with the rest of the class.

Matthew, a second grader, had IEP goals of learning to write his first and last name and to improve his handwriting by forming smaller letters and writing on the lines. Unfortunately, some handouts didn't contain a designated place to write his name and lines to write on. His teacher provided him with the same activities as his peers but infused them with opportunities to demonstrate his fine motor writing skills by designating a place for him to write his name on all his papers and adding lines or lined paper to all of his assignments.

The infused skills grid in figure 1.2 (page 25) helps determine how to incorporate goals and objectives during specific activities and classes. For instance, Bobby is a ninth-grade student with several occupational therapy goals. His sensory needs require him to have joint compressions three times daily. His initial schedule only allows for joint compressions twice daily; he needs one more session. His schedule indicates that he will enroll in a general education ninth-grade sports physical education class. After reviewing his infused skills grid and discussing creative ideas, Bobby's education team determines that he will enroll in a weight training physical education class instead. The weight machines naturally provide Bobby with the daily joint compressions that he needs.

Curriculum Overlapping

This approach doesn't change the curriculum but finds a way to combine resources or to use a single resource for more than one activity. This helps when the amount and depth of classroom tasks is daunting. Students can find it difficult to focus on several different subject areas, especially as they enter middle school and high school. As a result, curriculum overlapping allows students to work on an activity or assignment from one class in another.

For example, an eleventh grader named Susan must write a biography in U.S. history class and also must choose a book for independent reading in English class. Her teachers encourage her to choose a book about a U.S. historical figure as her independent reading book in English class. She no longer has to read two different books, which gives her more time and ability to focus on, and enjoy, her reading. Brian, another eleventh grader, has to create an interactive website in a web design course. He is simultaneously enrolled in an English class that requires creating a visual presentation on a novel recently read in class. Knowing that Brian needs additional time on his assignments and completing two projects would be difficult, his education team encourages him to create a website based on that novel. This is important for Brian because he often gives up on assignments when he feels very stressed or anxious. For Brian, overlapping the curriculum by creating one project for both classes allows him to successfully complete the assignment for English and web design and feel confident in himself. For some students, having to complete two different projects can be incredibly overwhelming. Also, they may need so much extended time to do both assignments that it makes sense to overlap the curriculum from two different classes.

Rigor

A common concern for educators is the misconception that adapting tasks waters down the curriculum and does not allow academic challenge. It is true that overuse of supports creates a restrictive learning environment and lessens the student's learning experience. However, underusing these supports also creates a restrictive learning environment as it limits student curriculum access and educational opportunities.

It is important to note that adapting learning tasks includes designing activities that will extend learning for those students who are ready. On the other hand, providing the scaffolds to the general education curriculum does not diminish rigor but instead allows the tools that best guide learning. Adaptations simply bridge the gap of skill development and facilitate understanding of the targeted learning standards.

In a true, responsive, systems thinking classroom, the objective for each student varies based on his or her performance level, meaning that measurable growth defines mastery. As students improve their performance, therefore, they demonstrate ongoing competency that may show their content knowledge and skill acquisition based on specific outlined targets. Instead of being concerned about whether the student can keep up with the rest of the class, focus is on his or her progress toward his or her specific goals. Rigor remains and the student still accomplishes the learning target as long as the appropriate structures support the necessary areas that allow the learning to continue. Continued growth can occur by maintaining high expectations that leverage effective adaptations all while aligning to individual student learning styles. Together, a student's educational team can ensure that the challenge remains in the lesson's rigor and does not obstruct the student's learning. In essence, if from the start educators prioritize quality instruction that is sensitive to the wide range of needs in the classroom, then students may have an opportunity to not only participate seamlessly but also to preserve knowledge. Remember that through collaboration, teachers bring their areas of expertise together, creating a balanced lesson with both differentiation and rigor.

Regardless of what adaptations teachers put in place, it is vital to maintain high expectations for all students within their ability level. This is especially true for learners who have difficulties with classwork since "teachers' expectations about their students affect students' opportunities to learn, their motivation, and their learning outcomes" (American Psychological Association, Coalition for Psychology in Schools and Education, 2015, p. 19).

How Can I Differentiate Instruction to Meet Students' Diverse Learning Needs?

If monitoring shows students are not making progress toward mastery, consider curriculum adaptations and instruction changes. This does not mean that students will work at a lower level, or that teachers dilute the curriculum; instead, appropriate changes put scaffolds into place that allow the student to meet high expectations. Rigor remains intact as long as a student is learning. For example, when Mark begins struggling with the writing process, his co-teachers provide him with supports such as sentence frames, graphic organizers, and peer tutors. The established curriculum is simply an outline of the content that students are expected to learn. The understanding that the academic standards set the bar and that the strategies, tools, and supports within a lesson provide access to that bar should drive lesson design.

Additionally, although it is vitally important that teachers address the struggles of individual learners, it is also critical that educators understand these challenges are situational. Struggling is not part of a student's identity. A student may have difficulties in one area that require supports, and the same student may be so successful in another area that he or she needs enrichment activities.

The Takeaways

Adaptations encompass both accommodations and modifications. Curriculum, technological, and environmental accommodations produce different supports for students who need them, and those accommodations are specific to each student, lessening over time if possible. Assessments for students who struggle must accurately portray their progress toward mastery, and so may require adaptation as well. However, accommodations are not restricted to students who have learning disabilities, because students with giftedness or twice-exceptionality need them as well for enrichment and extension. Regardless of why a student needs support, he or she can expect rigor as long as learning continues, and accommodations provide the necessary support. Avoid support overuse and ascertain the need for adaptation by growth. As long as growth continues, students are engaged in rigorous curriculum.

CHAPTER 3

DETERMINING PERSONAL SUPPORTS

Curriculum, technological, and environmental supports can only sometimes go so far as to help a student access curriculum. Some students need personal supports, which include full-time and part-time support staff, intermittent support staff, peer tutor support, natural supports, and supplemental supports (Fisher & Frey, 2015). The support staff members can be special educators, paraprofessionals, and health care personnel. Some students require considerable supports in terms of curriculum and personnel while others require less support. Teachers often have to investigate the available resources on campus.

Personal supports are fluid and flexible. Some students succeed with a variety of support staff, peer tutors, and natural supports depending on the class content, activities, projects, and task at hand. And like curriculum adaptations, teachers should gradually reduce personal supports as needed. Adult support can fade into peer tutor support. Peer tutor support can fade into natural supports.

It is critical to note that in our experience, regardless of the amount of support a student requires, the person providing that support should rotate with someone else. It is best practice to avoid assigning one personal support to one particular person for the whole day *or* every day. Consistency does have an impact, and it is important to have a routine; however, providing an array of individuals on a rotating basis reduces the risk of overdependence or burnout in any one student or personnel himself or herself.

The following sections define and discuss how teachers and other staff can most effectively provide different kinds of supports, including full-time, part-time, intermittent, peer tutor, natural, and supplemental supports. The text also discusses co-teaching.

Full-Time Support

The full-time support staff member is often in close proximity to the student and may assist with the direct instruction, materials, and supplies necessary to complete class assignments and group work. This level of support is often necessary for students with health needs, such as seizure disorders, or who require full-time oxygen, and for students who need behavioral support. This staff member also serves as a model for cooperation, collaboration, and respect in case of shaping positive behaviors. Depending on the students' needs, a full-time support staff person should *fade* (become less necessary and support less or less often) when possible, with the goal for the student to become increasingly independent. As he or she begins facilitating relationships between students with and without disabilities, it may allow for less direct support and increased intermittent or part-time support (Causton-Theoharis, 2009).

Part-Time Support

Part-time support staff members provide assistance at predetermined times or regularly check in on classrooms, providing an additional support in the classroom for a portion of the day. Part-time support might be all a student requires, but sometimes it could be the result of full-time support fading as the student learns the class's routines. Part-time support occurs more predictably than intermittent support, such as during the first fifteen minutes of a mathematics class or at the end of the day before dismissal. Part-time personnel support students academically and socially, ensuring they are active participants within the general education classroom.

Intermittent Support

Intermittent support is often flexible; students receive it on an as-needed basis that their curriculum, classroom activities, and needs dictate. For instance, teachers may schedule intermittent support when students are completing a science lab or test and require a scribe or small-group testing accommodation.

Michael, a second grader developing his English language skills, is an eager boy who loves participating with his peers in all classroom activities and being as independent as possible. However, depending on the task, he sometimes needs academic support to read materials, understand directions, and complete written work. For complex, detailed assignments or projects, his teacher arranges for an English learner instructor, special educator, or paraprofessional to be in the classroom. However, for the majority of the time, the teacher and Michael's peers within the classroom are able to support him.

Peer Tutor Support

Peer tutor support comes from other students. All students in a classroom have the ability to support each other. Peer support can be full time, part time, or intermittent.

Richard A. Villa and Jacqueline S. Thousand (2005) describe the act of helping each other in the classroom and building capacity among peers as twofold.

1. For the student who finds school tasks challenging, peer support results in academic growth and increased self-esteem.

2. The peer providing the support also reaps the benefit of strengthening his or her own learning and increasing self-esteem teaching the concept.

As Rachel Janney and Martha Snell (2013) explain, "Students can benefit, both academically and socially, from working together in shared activities, even if the objectives they accomplish within those activities are varied" (p. 146). Susana Jimenez, a high school paraprofessional, backs that insight with regard to peer supports:

> Peer support . . . [is] a great way to have students become more independent of an adult as their go-to person for help. When you establish these natural supports in the classroom, you feel more confident . . . you allow yourself to step back. Through peer support, students also begin to develop their social skills and hopefully end up with new friends. (personal communication, April 13, 2016)

Peer tutors, peer facilitators, or teaching assistants are a common support option in secondary schools. While not replacing the need for friends, tutors develop effective connections to other students. At the elementary level, this is often called a *buddy system*. Peers can assist with mobility, note taking, and facilitating group interactions.

At some middle and high schools, students can enroll as a peer tutor as part of an internship experience, career pathway, or an elective course managed by a lead support staff member, often a special educator. The tutors report to a special education teacher, receive a wide range of instruction, and complete related assignments. However, their main role is providing daily support to students who need additional guidance within the class. For example, Lauryn is a tenth-grade peer tutor who supports Kelly in the ninth-grade general education geography class. While Lauryn is not enrolled in that geography class herself, she does attend daily. She supports Kelly by reading aloud directions, clarifying questions, explaining tasks, and helping her follow along with class. Lauryn helps Kelly interact with peers and participate in group activities, and when Kelly is able to be independent during an activity, Lauryn fades her support and allows her peers to provide guidance as needed.

Tenth-grade English teacher Danielle Carlin says that peer support is one example of how including students in the general education classroom benefits every student (personal communication, April 1, 2016). Additionally, she explains, "Effective small-group instruction becomes far more possible when I have a dedicated peer tutor in the classroom. Furthermore, many students connect well with a peer tutor and will seek them out for academic assistance, creating a mentor-like relationship" (D. Carlin, personal communication, April 1, 2016). This type of relationship creates

a valuable impact that not only nourishes academic growth but facilitates the flour-
ishing of meaningful relationships that extend far beyond the classroom.

Natural Support

Support staff facilitate the natural supports that are available in the class. *Natural
supports* refer to students enrolled within the same classroom who are able to naturally provide guidance to each other as needed. This is in contrast to peer tutors, who
are assigned to the class to solely provide support. All students use natural supports
in a classroom as they assist one another. For instance, the teacher may assign pairs to
complete a particular assignment, which means peers will naturally supply support.
This requires the teacher to plan ahead and designate students who are most appropriate for the task. Every student, regardless of ability level, can lend a helping hand
to a peer and serve as an avenue of accessibility. Even students in elementary grades
are capable of providing assistance such as helping a classmate unpack a backpack,
get out school supplies, or turn in homework.

Effective teachers build in expectations about helping so it is part of the classroom
climate. When a student does not require structured full-time or part-time support,
he or she can easily rely on natural supports. If a student does not need continuous
support and the required level of support does not prevent peers from fully participating in class, try natural supports. Also, when support staff and peer tutors are
unavailable, natural supports can be a resource.

Supplemental Support

Supplemental support consists of related service personnel who provide their services within the general education classrooms. In collaboration with the general educator, these service providers can plan and develop optimal opportunities to meet
student needs within the general education curriculum and classroom activities. They
can even co-teach, benefiting all students. The special educator can assist in bringing
the general educators and related service personnel together. Ashlee Montferret, a
high school special educator who co-teaches and provides support in general education classrooms shares, "When related services are pushed into the classroom with
pre-planning with both the general and special educator, it can occur so naturally"
(personal communication, March 30, 2016).

Heather, a speech-language pathologist, always considers how she can implement
students' speech-language goals within the general education classroom. She also
emails teachers prior to her weekly classroom visits. Together, they determine ways
she can contribute to the lesson, to all students, and specifically to the students who
have speech-language goals. Other times, Heather and the general education teacher

meet in person. Heather always attends grade-level meetings and planning time at the school. Through this collaboration, Heather and the general education teachers plan what her involvement in the classroom will look like each day and how general educators can ensure that students are working on speech-language pathology goals even when Heather isn't in the classroom.

Co-Teaching

Richard A. Villa, Jacqueline S. Thousand, and Ann I. Nevin (2008) explain the strengths and differences of four co-teaching models: (1) team, (2) parallel, (3) complementary, and (4) supportive. Co-teaching can occur between two general educators or a general educator and special educator, related service provider, paraprofessional, peer tutor, or even a student.

Team co-teaching allows two people to teach the same lesson together, in tandem. Parallel co-teaching occurs when two individuals teach two separate groups of students by splitting the class in a variety of ways. Complementary co-teaching allows for one person to enhance the teaching provided by another. For example, while one person explains a concept, the other person writes the examples on the board. Lastly, supportive co-teaching consists of one person taking the lead designing and delivering instruction while the other person moves throughout the room supporting students as needed. It is important to note that the roles of instructor and classroom support should rotate between the two people.

Tenth-grade English teacher Danielle Carlin says of her experiences co-teaching:

> From the thought-provoking face-to-face planning to the energy and vitality it brings to the classroom, I enjoy the process entirely. This past year a special educator and I planned and presented a lesson connecting the Japanese internment camps in the U.S. during WWII to the Holocaust and current crises facing the world. The collaboration with the special educator took the lesson to another level, not only in its content, but also in the increased engagement of the students. Students were drawn in by hearing another voice, another perspective. Additionally, the academic discourse modeled between myself and the special educator raised that of the students as well. (personal communication, April 1, 2016)

Special educator Ashlee Montferret shares that co-teaching allows for combined expertise and smaller teacher-to-student ratios (personal communication, March 30, 2016). In addition, she says, "The planning portion is just as important as the teaching portion. It also makes me more confident in the general education content area. . . ." (A. Montferret, personal communication, March 30, 2016). When exploring and implementing the varieties of co-teaching, everyone involved develops a sense of belonging and commitment to the instructional process.

How Can I Leverage Structures to Improve Learning?

Building relationships, maintaining communication, being responsive, and promoting sustainability via systems thinking are key ways in which teachers can begin to improve the learning within their classrooms. Being in tune with students' individual needs creates an advantage that ensures teachers will reflect on and revamp their instructional styles to best serve all of these needs.

Educators should consider the following questions: How will incorporating universal design for learning principles in lesson planning and instruction facilitate all students' learning? How will providing the necessary adaptations provide greater access not just to students who struggle or students who are more advanced but the whole class? Can instructional activities cater to students by embedding strategies that involve whole-body movement, tactile activities, and collaborative group work? How can more engaging activities allow for natural supports to emerge?

A great example of incorporating breaks for K–5 classess is to give students the opportunity to act silly and release some energy during an hour-long mathematics block. After twenty-five minutes of learning how to add fractions with common denominators, the teacher can announce, "It's time to move. Slither like snakes for ten seconds and crawl like crabs for ten seconds." This movement activity gives all students a necessary brain break while attending to students who need extra physical movement to do their work. Everyone's attention and achievement increases with the breaks (Thurston, 2015). Moreover, since this is a consistent component within the classroom routine, the teacher seamlessly redirects the class back to the fractions lesson. In the same fashion, high school English co-teachers can embed five-minute phone breaks for their teenage students who, during instruction, constantly check their Snapchat, Instagram, and Twitter feeds or play online games.

The Takeaways

Personal supports come in a variety of iterations, including full time, part time, intermittent, peer tutor, natural, and supplemental. Co-teaching offers variations as well. Personal supports play a critical role in a systems thinking classroom. For instance, the relationship building and communication that occur when providing personal supports or while planning for co-teaching is extensive and adds an important layer to any classroom. All adaptations that teachers provide within a classroom must respond to students' individualized needs and learning styles, continuing to aim for sustainability that supports all students to transform from good to great.

CHAPTER 4

COMMUNICATING WITH KEY COLLABORATORS

Many variables play a role in ensuring students can access and master content. Crafting the content, process, and products for a systems thinking classroom requires teachers to establish a foundation based on relationships among students and education team members, including general and special education teachers, paraprofessionals, related service providers, students' families, and others. Collaboration among these groups can improve instruction. Each participant has a valuable perspective to contribute and offers knowledge and tools that build a stronger learning environment, including students. Villa, Thousand, and Nevin (2010) argue there are many rationales to collaborate with students, one of which is that "student collaboration increases academic and social competence" (p. 15). Overall, developing key relationships with all stakeholders involved in a student's education is imperative for student success in general education classrooms (Jones, 2012).

A strong focus on instructional strategies, data analysis, and progress monitoring helps all members of the education team accept responsibility and work toward improved performance for all students. For example, the tools discussed in chapter 1 (page 11)—the student profile, infused skills grid, and academic unit lesson plan— are products the education team members create in concert. Making these tools available for an entire team at a central location, such as a curriculum archive, improves co-planning efforts, since both general and special educators share responsibility for teaching students.

Tenth-grade English teacher Danielle Carlin embraces collaboration in her classroom:

> A special educator lends a perspective to planning which helps me to elevate my instruction by making its content truly accessible to all learners. This may be a task as simple as rearranging the format on a graphic organizer so that the information can be more easily recognized and understood. Yet this seemingly simple task may

make all the difference for a visual learner. (personal communication, April 1, 2016)

Fisher and Frey (2015) point out that "in a classroom, the systems we can leverage to improve learning include peer systems, curricular systems, and instructional systems . . . we adapt any and all of these to positively impact learning" (p. 128). All stakeholders must develop and use their capacity appropriately to endow students with the knowledge and, when applicable, adaptations that will allow them to flourish.

Villa and Thousand (2003) assert that fostering a quality learning environment for all students "takes both systems-level support and classroom-level strategies" (p. 19). Further, school leaders who understand and are steadfast in realizing this type of environment for all students report the following about collaboration in their schools: "If this collaborative, close-knit, supportive environment wasn't [here], the classrooms wouldn't be as inclusive" (Pineda Zapata, 2015). The underpinnings of inclusive school cultures consist of responsive leaders who understand the importance of effective communication and collaboration in building a sense of community that supports all learners.

The following sections explain key collaborators and how to best practice communication among them.

Naming Key Collaborators

Teachers should schedule and maintain communication with various stakeholders including classroom teachers (sometimes referred to as *general educators*), special educators, related service providers (sometimes referred to as *support providers*), paraprofessionals (sometimes referred to as *instructional assistants*), and other specialists (including English language instructors and reading specialists), students, and their families. Diligence in this vital area ensures that all team members are aware of student needs and the strategies that will best support students. The following sections outline who fits into these categories and how they collaborate to make a team.

General and Special Educators

Classroom teachers can be the primary leaders disseminating the vision for a particular lesson or unit. On a collaborative team, it is very likely different people will take the lead in certain processes. One teacher may coordinate communication among the rest of the team to develop a detailed student profile and infused skills grid, as well as ensure the team is aware of a student's learning needs and classroom activities. Another teacher may strategically coordinate the supports necessary for lesson delivery by developing the academic unit lesson plan. Regardless of who leads which area, all team members should understand that these roles are and should be fluid. The responsibility for all learners falls on the education team. Educators should meet face-to-face as a group as often as necessary to develop effective instruction and supports. Even if things are going well, it is important to regularly share progress and updates.

In addition to fulfilling these necessary roles, teachers have hopefully developed meaningful relationships with the students, which also aids in connecting the material with students' interests, background knowledge, and experiences. The special education teacher brings a unique set of abilities to the classroom that facilitates the design and implementation of necessary adaptations for all students. By collaborating, both the general education and special education teachers can anticipate possible barriers within a lesson and proactively structure their teaching approaches, content, and learning tasks to set the students up for success. Further, teachers can always furnish adaptations throughout the lesson as needed, however when both general education and special education teachers plan together from the beginning, they can execute their lesson delivery more seamlessly.

Paraprofessionals

Instructional assistants, or paraprofessionals, are integral in the classroom. They, too, should receive effective teaching strategies training, have a hand in developing instruction, and collaborate with the education team. Their role allows them to offer another perspective on how students learn and which students need support (versus which ones were possibly unengaged due to finishing early and needing an enrichment or extension task). Paraprofessionals are also integral to planning and implementation of co-teaching within an inclusive classroom setting. They can co-plan the lessons and provide the instruction alongside the classroom educator.

Related Service Providers

Related service providers, sometimes referred to as *supplemental services* or *support providers*, include but are not limited to individuals such as speech-language pathologists, counselors, psychologists, occupational therapists, physical therapists, assistive technology specialists, audiology specialists, mobility specialists, vision therapists, and deaf and hard-of-hearing specialists.

These professionals are also personal supports for a student since they apportion critical strategies and tools that empower and facilitate access to the learning environment. Consistent collaboration with each of these related service providers will ensure that teachers, paraprofessionals, students, and families are aware of what may be going on physically or psychologically in a particular student's life. Awareness of this information allows stakeholders to put the proper adaptations in place in and out of the classroom and to ensure needed skills in these specific areas are addressed daily, even when the specialists are not working directly with the students.

Students

It is logical to include students in the collaboration process. This is why meaningful relationships with students in the classroom are paramount. Make it a priority to become familiar with a student's learning style and preferences. Converse with them. Focus the conversations, as naturally as possible, on a student's favorite reading genre; whether he or she learns best in a small group or with a peer; if he or she can see the board and hear the teacher from where he or she sits; what difficulties he or she had with a particular assignment; which graphic organizer helped his or her writing the most and whether more examples would help. Teachers can inquire about these topics individually, face-to-face, or through periodic surveys. Then they can include the information they collect in the student profile and the academic unit lesson plan.

Teachers should hear and respect students' voices. They can provide insights about what engages them and what helps them and their peers learn best. Metacognition is another benefit of including students in these discussions. They learn to reflect on which adaptations they need to succeed and communicate about them. Educational team members can help students advocate for themselves. Providing students with a list of their adaptations helps them communicate this with teachers and staff as needed. Staff should encourage students to practice asking for help and advocating for their needs by using sentence frames such as, "I know we have a test coming up, so I will need the following supports . . . ."

Students who know what they need and who can share this information are experiencing success. Teachers can also invite students to give input on an upcoming lesson or project to increase buy-in and improve the lesson's efficacy and impact. Arturo Cuevas, a tenth-grade mathematics teacher, requested feedback on the previous lesson he had given and asked students to provide suggestions for how he could organize the upcoming collaborative group project (personal communication, April 1, 2016). Other teachers may invite students they have had in prior years to collaborate with them on projects and assignments for the current year. Prior-year students would then provide feedback on what parts of the lesson or project were engaging and thought provoking, as well as which parts seemed cumbersome and confusing. In this way, teachers can use prior student experiences to continuously improve instruction. Similarly, classroom peers may offer creative ways to support their fellow students. This consideration is especially critical if they are peer tutors or have acted as natural supports. Accordingly, teachers may share information with peers when they deem necessary with deep consideration for confidentiality.

Families

Families need to know that teachers are invested in their children's success. Building relationships with families can make a difference. For example, when interviewing a number of principals from successful inclusive schools, Yazmin Pineda Zapata (2015) finds that school principals prioritize opportunities to educate families and value their input because it allows school staff to learn about the aspirations the families have for their children. If families trust their children's teachers, they are more apt to share information that can be useful in ensuring success.

Research shows that when schools encourage and motivate families to actively participate in their children's education, the children succeed. Indeed, a home and school partnership yields higher test scores and graduation rates, improves school attendance and behavior, and leads to a higher likelihood of college attendance (Epstein, 2010; Henderson & Berla, 1994). This vital partnership develops a shared responsibility among the education team members and the family. Work to create a seamless connection and environment of genuine care across home and school.

The National Parent Teacher Association (n.d.) says these six standards of family involvement are present in a home and school partnership.

1. Welcoming, valuing, and engaging all families into the school community

2. Communicating effectively both ways

3. Supporting family efforts to encourage student learning at home and at school

4. Advocating for every student

5. Affording families the occasion to participate in school decision making

6. Increasing community involvement

It is important that families have opportunities to engage with a variety of school members and a consistent avenue of communication with their children's education teams. Parents know the student best and are valuable resources for education teams; therefore, their input should be included on the student profile. Inviting parents to contribute key information about students not only helps teachers build meaningful relationships with students, but provides information teachers can use to design instruction. Teachers may attain this useful information through a variety of communications, including but not limited to parent-teacher conferences, parent surveys, daily communication (such as communication logs or emails), and IEP meetings. Families should have communication access to administrators, teachers, paraprofessionals, related service providers, counselors, and others such as school bus drivers if applicable. Facilitate parent knowledge about standards, curricula, and adaptations. Teachers can only guarantee families that their participation makes a difference when they are full and equal partners.

Sharing Responsibility

Although many school and community members influence a student's education experience, general and special education teachers, as well as other specialists, are the primary liaisons that facilitate learning and provide instructional and personal support within a classroom. Again, although one teacher may take the lead on certain tasks, the process is always collaborative. Implement consistently shared decision making. Creating a lesson plan that meets the needs of all learners is the priority for strategic co-planning and collaboration among key education team members.

High school biology teacher Kim Elliot explains her role as a general educator with shared responsibility:

> My role in collaborating with the special educator serves as the content expert and the lead in planning how to deliver instruction. The special educator is the expert on providing adaptations of the lesson's material as well as offering instructional strategies that can augment a lesson. (personal communication, April 1, 2016)

High school mathematics teacher Joseph Assof agrees and emphasizes how essential both teachers are in the classroom: "Special educators bring not only different eyes, but a different lens, into the classroom that clarifies . . . what a modification or accommodation truly is" (personal communication, May 20, 2016).

Through collaboration and shared responsibility, teachers pool their expertise to create a lesson with both differentiation and rigor. As an example, specialists may take the lead on speaking to all general education teachers, families, and other related service providers to gain critical information for a student profile. Similarly, the general education teacher may want to take the lead for a student who is not receiving special education services or one who is currently receiving intervention for academic struggles or language development. Therefore, the general education teacher may want to develop this particular student profile to determine strategies in collaboration with the specialists.

In another instance, the special education teacher, reading specialist, or English language instructor may take the lead on identifying the goals and objectives for a student's infused skills grid. But the team, including the general education teacher and other pertinent staff, collaboratively discusses how to address, within the student's daily schedule, the skills for these goals and objectives. On the other hand, the general education teacher may take the lead on identifying target standards, lesson objectives, and key activities using the academic unit lesson plan, but co-plan with the appropriate specialists to collaboratively determine appropriate adaptations for individual students.

When educators make honest attempts at sharing the lead, they create shared ownership of all students' learning, where they can feel comfortable releasing traditional role definitions and maximizing the learning environment. Accordingly, regardless of position or title, educators ensure the proper systems are in place for each child. Discuss them as *our students*, never as *your students* or *my students*. This simple shift in language can dramatically change views and the culture. The following driving questions can ensure that this process takes place and that a systems thinking approach is firmly established.

- Have I taken the time to learn about my students via their student profiles?

- Have I collaborated with *all* stakeholders on how to best meet individual students' needs?

- Have *we* built a relationship of open communication with students and their families, as well as with each other?

- Have *we* used universal design for learning principles to ensure that instructional delivery meets the varying needs in the classroom?

- In collaboration with all involved, have *we* used the tools (student profile, infused skills grid, academic unit lesson plan, and IEP) necessary to adequately design a well-structured lesson with the appropriate adaptations?

- Have *we* explored each component of the triangle of support to determine need in any of these areas?

- Have *we* used available personal resources?

- Have *we* explored all options for necessary technological supports?

- Have *we* provided all adaptations for classroom activities, assignments, and assessments?

Creating time for co-planning and creating a curriculum archive are indispensable collaboration components.

Co-planning

Educators must create time to co-plan. However, with classroom and committee demands, finding this time is difficult, so it's necessary to be creative to carve it out. Because time is such a limited resource, it is all the more reason for teachers and staff to combine resources and communicate responsively about what they have already invested time in. Teachers have found time to co-plan lessons in the following places and times.

How:

- In person

- Via email or text

- Via shared online materials

When:

- Before school

- Lunch

- Prep periods

- Grade-level and subject-area team meetings
- After school

Where:

- Faculty lounge
- Classrooms
- Any other appropriate location on campus

Some teachers prefer face-to-face interaction, where they can ask questions and bounce ideas off others. These teams must decide an exact day and time to meet. This may occur before school, during lunch, during a prep period, or after school. Some teachers use the time during specific daytime activities (such as art or library) if another teacher or staff member is teaching the class, in the lounge, and even between class periods. Include the special educator, paraprofessionals, and related support providers in grade-level and content-area team meetings.

Some educators prefer brief in-person collaborations along with making more extensive arrangements online. This may occur through emails with pertinent lessons and activities as attachments or with online storage and sharing of materials. Online options or dual access to the classroom learning management system makes sharing curriculum simple and easy. All teachers can then suggest adaptations directly in the lesson or activity itself.

Co-planning is when everyone decides who is doing what. This communication helps teachers avoid creating adaptations that repeat those of other staff members. Treat personal supports, curriculum adaptations, and technology adaptations as guideposts to address all areas of need. Best practices dictate an electronic storage system that works for each educator and sharing these documents with a student's entire education team. When all staff members have access, they can share the adaptations they have created to save time for others.

To assist staff who are unfamiliar with the classroom content and who will adapt tasks and materials, provide answer keys for in-class activities, assignments, and assessments as needed. These staff may not have background knowledge in that content area.

During co-planning, the team decides who is responsible for maintaining the curriculum archive.

Curriculum Archive

A *curriculum archive* is a physical or virtual place where all versions of the adapted curriculum are stored. The archive can be paper copies in a filing cabinet, electronic copies on the cloud, or an online management system. Retaining all versions of the curriculum allows teachers to reuse what they need. It can be smoother to change an already adapted assignment. Nevertheless, there is no adaptation panacea. Regardless of how many adapted versions an educator has, sometimes a student requires a new version since designing adaptations always considers individualized student needs.

Have I Checked the Results of My Curriculum and Instruction and Taken Action to Ensure Successive Approximation?

If a student does not progress as he or she should, it urges teachers to re-evaluate their systems thinking approach and how they design and incorporate the most relevant adaptations for that particular student. It behooves teachers to continually reflect and act within the four components of the systems thinking approach, consider the relationships that are linked to this student, and include other members of the education team. This then requires the educators to communicate and discuss what other specific supports and strategies may help the student succeed. Additionally, consulting with the family, a valuable part of the education team, could reveal situations that may have influenced assessment results and school behavior. When educators redesign instruction and talk with all stakeholders, they are intentionally responding to student needs and therefore creating a sustainable environment that prioritizes the student as a whole person.

We caution educators to ensure *access to learning* versus just *access to information*. This requires careful planning so that students do not just receive data but also the tools and strategies they need to comprehend what teachers are presenting. The education team mindfully chooses materials, instructional methods, and assessment strategies.

The Takeaways

Collaboration among all education team members is crucial to providing the necessary adaptations to ensure student success. Key team members include the general and special education teachers, paraprofessionals, related service providers, the students themselves, and their families. The systems thinking approach of communicating and building relationships, as well as remaining responsive and creating sustainability, is paramount to this co-planning and collaboration. A stored curriculum archive of all adaptation iterations is a good resource for the future.

Changing a Belief System

The concept of a systems thinking approach is intertwined in every aspect of developing lessons according to universal design for learning principles and activities that provide access to all learners. Developing a systems thinking classroom requires education practitioners to reflect and commit themselves to taking the challenges that students face and using them to create an environment where they can help meet student needs. Responsive educators consider the existence of communication barriers and varying learning styles as opportunities to dive into collaborative and innovative lesson design. Collaboration among education teams—the co-planned lessons, universal design for learning principles, support system, student profile, infused skills grid, and academic unit lesson plan—removes the barriers.

We advocate for educators to rigorously question their instructional models and evaluate their belief systems and actions. It is vital that educators redefine their views and eschew low expectations for students who have difficulties. Consider each viewpoint. How can a student show competence if he or she does not have the necessary tools to develop those skills? What impedes a particular student from demonstrating knowledge? Is it a physical or language barrier that requires support to overcome or has he or she never learned a prerequisite skill? Has the instruction failed to address specific learning styles? Has the student accessed all available resources? Has there been an opportunity to establish specific learning criteria for individual students? Have the assessments and progress-monitoring activities facilitated student growth based on individual learning objectives?

The solution lies in a mindset that believes promoting student learning with appropriate supports is central to the success of all students. When educators believe all students have a right to high-quality learning opportunities, they proactively incorporate individual student cultures, languages, and experiences into their instruction. Take the brave step of attributing a student's lower performance to the need for improved instructional methods, not to the student him- or herself. Cheryl Jorgensen

(2005) reminds educators that "all people have different talents and skills" and that students "learn best when they feel valued, when [educators] hold high expectations for them, and when they are taught and supported well" (p. 7). In this paradigm, teachers see students as capable of learning. They focus on strengths and abilities. Assuming a student is capable of learning far outweighs the consequences of denying that student the opportunity to meet high expectations.

What Are the Short- and Long-Term Consequences of the Adaptations I Provide for Students?

To thoroughly investigate this question, educators must consider questions like these: What will students gain in a small amount of time if they receive adaptations to their learning environment and curriculum? What long-term results are students and educators striving for and how will they monitor them? Will this particular adaptation hold them to high expectations and involve rigor? Is a support providing independence or halting it? What is the plan for fading adaptations?

An education team determines its expectations for the short and long term in regard to accommodations and modifications. Those expectations provide a framework for effective monitoring. It is critical that these adaptations are not just provided and left alone. Monitor constantly and adjust teaching approaches daily. Reflect on whether curriculum is accessible and therefore equitable, and proactively adjust these supports to address *all* students' individualized needs.

References and Resources

American Psychological Association, Coalition for Psychology in Schools and Education. (2015). *Top 20 principles from psychology for preK–12 teaching and learning.* Accessed at www.apa.org/ed/schools/cpse/top-twenty-principles.pdf on September 28, 2016.

Burgstahler, S. (2015). *Universal design of instruction (UDI): Definition, principles, guidelines, and examples.* Accessed at www.washington.edu/doit/universal-design-instruction-udi-definition-principles-guidelines-and-examples on September 28, 2016.

California Services for Technical Assistance and Training. (2013). Universal design for learning: What it is, what it looks like, where to learn more. *The Special Edge, 26*(1), 2–3.

Castagnera, E., Fisher, D., Rodifer, K., Sax, C., & Frey, N. (2003). *Deciding what to teach and how to teach it: Connecting students through curriculum and instruction* (2nd ed.). Colorado Springs, CO: PEAK Parent Center.

Causton-Theoharis, J. (2009). *The paraprofessional's handbook for effective support in inclusive classrooms.* Baltimore: Brookes.

Center for Applied Special Technology. (2011). *Universal design for learning guidelines, version 2.0.* Wakefield, MA: Author. Accessed at www.udlcenter.org/aboutudl/udlguidelines on August 16, 2016.

Connell, B. R., Jones, M., Mace, R., Mueller, J., Mullick, A., Ostroff, E., et al. (1997). *The principles of universal design: Version 2.0.* Accessed at www.ncsu.edu/ncsu/design/cud/about_ud/udprinciplestext.htm on September 28, 2016.

Crockett, J. B. (2011). Conceptual models for leading and administrating special education. In J. M. Kauffman & D. P. Hallahan (Eds.), *Handbook of special education* (pp. 351–362). New York: Routledge.

Curwin, R. L., & Mendler, A. N. (1988). *Discipline with dignity.* Alexandria, VA: Association for Supervision and Curriculum Development.

Dolan, R. P., Hall, T. E., Banerjee, M., Chun, E., & Strangman, N. (2005). Applying principles of universal design to test delivery: The effect of computer-based read-aloud on test performance of high school students with learning disabilities. *Journal of Technology, Learning, and Assessment, 3*(7). Accessed at https://ejournals.bc.edu/ojs/index.php/jtla/article/download/1660/1496 on December 16, 2016.

Education for All Handicapped Children Act, Pub. L. No. 94-142, § 89 Stat., 773 (1975).

Elementary and Secondary Education Act of 1965, Pub. L. No. 89-10, § 79 Stat., 27 (1965).

Epstein, J. L. (2010). Caring connections. *Phi Delta Kappan*, 92(3), 65.

Every Student Succeeds Act, Pub. L. No. 114-95, § 114 Stat., 1177 (2015).

Fisher, D., & Frey, N. (2015). *Unstoppable learning: Seven essential elements to unleash student potential.* Bloomington, IN: Solution Tree Press.

Gaines, K. S., & Curry, Z. D. (2011). The inclusive classroom: The effects of color on learning and behavior. *Journal of Family and Consumer Sciences Education*, 29(1), 46–57.

Hall, T. E., Meyer, A., & Rose, D. H. (Eds.). (2012). *Universal design for learning in the classroom: Practical applications.* New York: Guilford Press.

Hall, T. E., Vue, G., Strangman, N., & Meyer, A. (2014). *Differentiated instruction and implications for UDL implementation.* Wakefield, MA: National Center on Accessing the General Curriculum. Accessed at http://aem.cast.org/about/publications/2003/ncac-differentiated-instruction-udl.html on February 23, 2017.

Hattie, J. (2012). *Visible learning for teachers: Maximizing impact on learning.* London: Routledge.

Henderson, A. T. & Berla, N. (Eds.). (1994). *A new generation of evidence: The family is critical to student achievement.* Columbia, MD. National Committee for Citizens in Education.

Hunt, J. H., & Andreasen, J. B. (2011). Making the most of universal design for learning. *Mathematics Teaching in the Middle School, 17*(3), 166–172.

Janney, R. & Snell, M. E. (2013). *Modifying schoolwork: Teachers' guides to inclusive practices* (3rd ed.). Baltimore: Brooks.

Jones, B. A. (2012). Fostering collaboration in inclusive settings: The special education students at a glance approach. *Intervention in School and Clinic, 47*(5), 297–306.

Jorgensen, C. (2005). The least dangerous assumption: A challenge to create a new paradigm. *Disability Solutions, 6*(3), 1, 5–9, 15.

Knez, I. (2014). Affective and cognitive reactions to subliminal flicker from fluorescent lighting. *Consciousness and Cognition, 26*(1), 97–104.

Meyer, A., & Rose, D. H. (2005). The future is in the margins: The role of technology and disability in educational reform. D. H. Rose, A. Meyer, & C. Hitchcock (Eds.), *The universally designed classroom: Accessible curriculum and digital technologies* (pp. 13–35). Cambridge, MA: Harvard Education Press.

Meyer, A., Rose, D. H., & Gordon, D. (2014). *Universal design for learning: Theory and practice.* Wakefield, MA: Center for Applied Special Technology.

Moody, C. J. (2014). *Expert-recommended strategies for teaching the twice-exceptional student in the general education classroom* (Doctoral dissertation). Accessed at ProQuest. (3584991).

Myler, P. A., Fantacone, T. A., & Merritt, E. T. (2003, November). Eliminating distractions: The educational needs of autistic children challenge ordinary approaches to school design. *American School and University.* Accessed at http://asumag.com/accessibility/eliminating-distractions on November 30, 2016.

National Association for Gifted Children. (n.d.). *Twice-exceptionality* [White paper]. Accessed at www.nagc.org/sites/default/files/Position%20Statement/twice%20exceptional.pdf on November 30, 2016.

National Governors Association Center for Best Practices & Council of Chief State School Officers. (2010). *Common Core State Standards for English language arts and literacy in history/social studies, science, and technical subjects*. Washington, DC: Authors. Accessed at www.corestandards.org/assets/CCSSI_ELA%20Standards.pdf on March 12, 2017.

National Parent Teacher Association. (n.d.). *National standards for family-school partnerships*. Accessed at www.pta.org/nationalstandards on January 11, 2017.

Obeidat, A., & Al-Share, R. (2012). Quality learning environments: Design-studio classroom. *Asian Culture and History*, *4*(2), 165–174.

Pineda Zapata, Y. (2015.) *A principal's role in creating and sustaining an inclusive environment*. (Unpublished doctoral dissertation). San Diego State University, San Diego, CA.

Roberson, R. (2013, September). *Helping students find relevance: Teaching the relevance of course content can help students develop into engaged, motivated and self-regulated learners*. American Psychological Association. Accessed at www.apa.org/ed/precollege/ptn/2013/09/students-relevance.aspx on May 8, 2017.

Shepherd, K., & Hasazi, S. B. (2008). Leadership for social justice and inclusion. In L. Florian (Ed.), *The SAGE handbook of special education* (pp. 475–485). Los Angeles: SAGE.

Stokes, S. (n.d.). *Structured teaching: Strategies for supporting students with autism?* Accessed at www.cesa7.org/sped/autism/structure/str10.htm on November 30, 2016.

Teven, J. J., & McCroskey, J. C. (1997). The relationship of perceived teacher caring with student learning and teacher evaluation. *Communication Education*, *46*(1), 1–9.

Thurston, A. (2015, Summer). Moving to improve. *@SED Magazine*, 7–9. Accessed at www.bu.edu/sed/files/2015/07/SED_Spring15_Final.pdf on December 1, 2016.

Tilton, L. (2001). *Inclusion: A fresh look — Practical strategies to help all students succeed* (5th ed). Shorewood, MN: Covington Cove.

Tomlinson, C. A. (2014). *The differentiated classroom: Responding to the needs of all learners* (2nd ed). Alexandria, VA: Association for Supervision and Curriculum Development.

VanTassel-Baska, J., & Stambaugh, T. (2005). Challenges and possibilities for serving gifted learners in the regular classroom. *Theory Into Practice*, *44*(3), 211–217.

Villa, R. A., & Thousand, J. S. (2003). Making inclusive education work. *Educational Leadership*, *61*(2), 19–23.

Villa, R. A., & Thousand, J. S. (Eds.). (2005). *Creating an inclusive school* (2nd ed.). Alexandria, VA: Association for Supervision and Curriculum Development.

Villa, R. A., Thousand, J. S., & Nevin, A. I. (2008). *A guide to co-teaching: Practical tips for facilitating student learning* (2nd ed.). Thousand Oaks, CA: Corwin Press.

Villa, R. A., Thousand, J. S., & Nevin, A. I. (2010). *Collaborating with students in instruction and decision making: The untapped resource*. Thousand Oaks, CA: Corwin Press.

WebAIM. (2013). *Constructing a POUR website: Putting people at the center of the process*. Accessed at http://webaim.org/articles/pour on September 28, 2016.

Winterbottom, M., & Wilkins, A. J. (2009). Lighting and discomfort in the classroom. *Journal of Environmental Psychology*, *29*(1), 63–75.

Index

A

academic unit lesson plan, 18, 21–22, 27–28
accessibility, 36
accommodations
    adaptations as, 47–49
    assessment, 41–46
    curriculum, 33–35
    defined, 1–2, 33
    environmental, 39–40
    for those who have giftedness and twice-
        exceptionality, 40–41
    meaningful, 36
    technology, 35–39
action (intake) and expression, 17–18
adaptations, 1
    See also accommodations; modifications
    changing, 69–70
    questions to ask, 14, 32
    reviewing, 67
    types of, 31
adapting learning, defined, 1–2
Al-Share, R., 39
Arnaiz, B., 19
assessment accommodations, 41–46
Assof, J., 64

B

breaks, providing, 58
buddy system, 55

C

Carlin, D., 19, 55, 57, 59–60
Castagnera, E., 18, 21, 22
Center for Applied Special Technology (CAST),
    16–17

Center for Universal Design (CUD), 16
collaboration
    co-planning, 65–66
    role of, 59–60
    shared responsibility, 63–65
    students and, 62
collaborators
    paraprofessionals (instructional assistants),
        60, 61
    service (support) providers, 60, 61
    special educators, 60–61
    specialists, 60, 61
    teachers (general educators), 60–61
communication, 5
    role of, 12–13
    tools, 37
compacted curriculum, 40
complementary co-teaching, 57
complexity, 32
computer adaptations, 37–38
Connell, B. R., 17
co-planning, 65–66
co-teaching, 57
Cuevas, A., 62
curriculum accommodations, 33–35
curriculum adaptations, 3, 4, 15
curriculum archive, 66–67
curriculum overlapping, 49
curriculum, streamlined, 47–48
Curry, Z. D., 39
Curwin, R. L., 1

D

differentiated instruction, 13–15, 18, 32, 40, 50
difficulty, 32

E

Education for All Handicapped Children Act
    (1975), xi
educational aids, 37
Elementary and Secondary Education Act
    (1965), xi
Elliot, K., 19, 64
engagement, 18
enrichment activities, 40
environmental accommodations, 39–40
equity versus equality, 1, 7
essays, 44
Every Student Succeeds Act (ESSA) (2015), xi
extension activities, 40

F

fading, 54
families, relationships with, 62–63
fill-in-the-blank questions, 43
fine and gross motor supports, 37
Fisher, D., 2, 3, 8, 11–12, 31, 40, 47, 60
Frey, N., 2, 3, 8, 11–12, 31, 40, 47, 60

G

Gaines, K. S., 39
generalization, 20
gifted, 8, 33, 40–41
Google Drive, 39

H

Hall, T. E., 7, 13
Hattie, J., 22
high-tech supports, 15, 36–39

I

individualized education plans (IEPs), 19, 20,
    46, 48
infused skills grid, 18, 20–21, 25–26, 48
input, 4, 36
instructional assistants (paraprofessionals), role
    of, 60, 61

J

Janney, R., 55
Jimenez, S., 20, 35, 55
Jorgensen, C., 69–70

K

Knez, I., 39

L

learning tools, 18–28
low-tech supports, 15, 36–39

M

matching, 43–44
mathematics frames, 45
McCroskey, J. C., 12
Mendler, A. N., 1
Meyer, A., 7, 13, 18
modifications
    adaptations as, 47–49
    defined, 1–2
    role of, 46–47
Montferret, A., 19, 56, 57
Moody, C., 41
multiple choice, 42
multitiered system of supports (MTSS), 13, 19

N

National Association for Gifted Children
    (NAGC), 40–41
National Center on Universal Design for
    Learning, 17
National Parent Teacher Association, 63
natural support, 56
Nevin, A. I., 57, 59

O

Obeidat, A., 39
output, 4, 36

P

parallel co-teaching, 57
parallel problems, 45
paraprofessionals (instructional assistants), role
    of, 60, 61
peer tutor support, 54–56
personal supports
    co-teaching, 57
    full-time, 53–54
    intermittent, 54
    natural, 56
    part-time, 54
    peer tutor, 54–56
    role of, 3, 4, 15, 33
    supplemental, 56–57
    types of, 53
Pineda Zapata, Y., 62–63
Pocket, 39

R

Read&Write for Google Chrome, 39
relationships, 5, 12
    with families, 62–63
    with students, 62
representation, 17
response to instruction and intervention (RTI²),
        13, 19
responsibility, shared, 63–65
responsiveness, 5, 13–14
rigor, 49–50
Rose, D. H., 7, 18

S

same, only less, 47
same activity with infused objective, 48
scaffolding, 18, 33
service (support) providers, role of, 60, 61
shared responsibility, 63–65
Snell, M., 55
special educators, role of, 60–61
standards, 32
Strangman, N., 13
streamlined curriculum, 47–48
student profile, 18–20, 23–24
students, collaboration and relationships with, 62
study guides, 45
supplemental services, 61
support. *See* personal supports; triangle of
        support
support providers, role of, 60, 61
supportive co-teaching, 57
sustainability, 5, 14
systems thinking
    defined, 2–3, 11–12
    description of, 11–14
    melding of, 5–6
    principles of, 5, 12–14

T

teachers, role of, 60–61
team co-teaching, 57
technology, instructional and assistive, 3, 4, 15
technology accommodations (supports), 35–39
Teven, J. J., 12
Thousand, J. S., 55, 57, 59, 60
Tilton, L., 34–35, 42, 43, 48
Tomlinson, C. A., 13
triangle of support, components of, 3–4, 15

true or false questions, 43
twice-exceptional learners, 8, 33, 40–41

U

universal design for learning
    background of, 15–16
    components of, 17–18
    defined, 4–5, 6, 17
    principles of, 16–17
    tools, 18–28
Unstoppable Learning, components of, 2–3
Unstoppable Learning (Fisher and Frey), 2, 3, 8,
        31, 47
usability, 36

V

Villa, R. A., 55, 57, 59, 60

W

Web Accessibility in Mind (WebAIM), 38–39
websites, 38–39

Unstoppable Learning
Douglas Fisher and Nancy Frey

Discover proven methods to enhance teaching and learning schoolwide. Identify questions educators should ask to guarantee a positive classroom culture where students learn from each other, not just teachers. Explore ways to adapt teaching in response to students' individual needs.

BKF662

A Handbook for Unstoppable Learning
Laurie Robinson Sammons and Nanci N. Smith

Learn how to foster effective teaching and deep learning using the seven elements of the Unstoppable Learning model. Gain access to templates for planning learning targets, assessments, lessons, and units that will help create and maintain positive, healthy, high-performing classrooms.

BKF775

Think Big, Start Small
Gayle Gregory and Martha Kaufeldt

You don't have to be a neuroscientist to understand how your students absorb knowledge. This easy-to-understand guide pares down the vast field of neuroscience and provides simple brain-compatible strategies that will make a measurable difference in your differentiated classroom.

BKF471

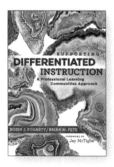

Supporting Differentiated Instruction
Robin J. Fogarty and Brian M. Pete

Examine how PLCs provide the decision-making platform for the rigorous work of differentiated classroom instruction. A practical guide to implementing differentiation in the classroom, this book offers a road map to effective teaching that responds to diverse learning needs.

BKF348

Solution Tree | Press
a division of

Solution Tree

Visit SolutionTree.com or call 800.733.6786 to order.

Wait! Your professional development journey doesn't have to end with the last pages of this book.

We realize improving student learning doesn't happen overnight. And your school or district shouldn't be left to puzzle out all the details of this process alone.

No matter where you are on the journey, we're committed to helping you get to the next stage.

Take advantage of everything from **custom workshops** to **keynote presentations** and **interactive web and video conferencing**. We can even help you develop an action plan tailored to fit your specific needs.

Let's get the conversation started.

Call 888.763.9045 today.